PLUS

3095 PLUS

OHIO'S FALLEN
The Battle for a Veterans' Memorial

ERIN LYNN RADER   KENNETH C. NOON

3095 Plus: Ohio's Fallen © Copyright <<2025>> ErinLynnRader

All rights reserved. No part of this publication may be reproduced, distributed or transmitted in any form or by any means, including photocopying, recording, or other electronic or mechanical methods, without the prior written permission of the publisher, except in the case of brief quotations embodied in critical reviews and certain other noncommercial uses permitted by copyright law.

Although the author and publisher have made every effort to ensure that the information in this book was correct at press time, the author and publisher do not assume and hereby disclaim any liability to any party for any loss, damage, or disruption caused by errors or omissions, whether such errors or omissions result from negligence, accident, or any other cause.

Adherence to all applicable laws and regulations, including international, federal, state and local governing professional licensing, business practices, advertising, and all other aspects of doing business in the U.S., Canada or any other jurisdiction is the sole responsibility of the reader and consumer.

Neither the author nor the publisher assumes any responsibility or liability whatsoever on behalf of the consumer or reader of this material. Any perceived slight of any individual or organization is purely unintentional.

The truth is reported as accurately as it possibly can be by the writer. The text covers more than two decades; memories of the participants can be faulty. There are always disagreements in such a story told by many people involved in the same project; there may be conflicting memories as well. The writer makes no judgment on these issues. The reader may if they wish.

Neither the author nor the publisher can be held responsible for the psychological effect of the information within this book. Please always consult a trained professional before making any decision regarding treatment of yourself or others.

For more information, email SBN: raderin@gmail.com.

ISBN: 979-8-89694-389-1 - Ebook

ISBN: 979-8-89694-390-7 - Paperback

ISBN: 979-8-89694-391-4 - Hardcover

For Duke

Contents

Prologue 1
Foreword 5
Preface 9
Chapter One 15
Chapter Two 31
Chapter Three 53
Chapter Four 77
Chapter Five 95
Chapter Six 123
Chapter Seven 151
Chapter Eight 175
Chapter Nine 201
Notes 233
Acknowledgements 241
Thank You For Reading Our Book 243

Prologue

The motorcycles were coming soon, and Ken Noon walked the gravel lot overlooking the imposing black granite wall. For Ken, a stone-sculpting artist, and for the veterans who designed it, the first sight of the park was crucial. Today, he was there to ensure the riders had an unobstructed view.

A car blocked the main drive at the ring road that wound around the pristine monuments bearing the names of the honored dead. As Ken approached the driver to ask him to move, he was taken aback by the sight of the distraught man behind the wheel. The man was sobbing, shoulders shaking, trying to pull himself together when he saw Ken approach. With some effort, he began to share his story.

For years, he and his wife had noticed the Ohio Veterans Memorial Park sign on the highway. They wondered if it was a state park, since it was a small brown-and-white sign. The man, a veteran himself, thought of stopping by every time they passed but always had somewhere else to be. His wife would remind him, "It's just in tiny Clinton—what could possibly be there? A statue? An inscribed granite block? It wouldn't be worth the time, and you'd be disappointed."

The man cried, and Ken waited patiently. Grown men crying at the monument was something he'd seen many times before.

"My curiosity got the best of me today, so we came. Thank God," the man said, sniffing and wiping his eyes. He glanced down the slope at the gleaming 125-foot-long black monument, inscribed with the names of 3,095 Ohioans who had given their lives in Southeast Asia.

He asked if the name of a friend who had been killed in Vietnam was on the wall. Ken replied that it probably was. The man's head dropped as he sobbed again.

The wall gleamed, and the golden words "Lest We Forget" at the top flashed in the sun. He had not forgotten. But how he wished he had come sooner, to honor his friend before today. The man lived only a thirty-minute drive away, but he simply hadn't known this place was here.

Clinton is a small village, the third smallest in Summit County, Ohio, with just 1,100 residents. Its picturesque downtown is home to a village hall, a busy drive-through beverage store with a covered bridge façade, an auto shop, a realty office, and a fire station. Police services are shared with a nearby city. The post office, perched on a hill a block away, flies an American flag. Throughout the village, flags wave in the breeze, symbols of the town's patriotism. Nearby are a beautiful lake, a park, and the Ohio and Erie Canal Towpath. Across from the Methodist church lies a lovely cemetery, set against the lakeshore and central to this story, the Clinton Cemetery.

This was not the obvious choice for a stately and serene veterans' park, yet it was the perfect spot—destined. It became the passion project of a handful of veterans with a big dream and no funds.

This is a story of courage, valor, and service—of honoring brethren and country. It is a story of the men and one woman whose names are etched on the front of that wall, and those on the other side: the other front. And of the veterans and volunteers who built and continue to care for these stunning grounds.

Prologue

This is a story spanning two decades:

Of the good and the bad.
Of challenges, struggles, and perseverance.
Of those who got along, and those who didn't.
Of those who argued and left, and those who argued and stayed.
Of difficult decisions, long days, and longer nights.
Of physical, emotional, and financial sacrifice.

It is a story of pure joy when dreams were realized, and of the satisfaction of seeing hundreds turn out to honor those commemorated. It is a story of grieving and healing.

It is a story told by those who built the incredible monuments, and by those who were on the battlefields. It is told for their families. It is told for and dedicated to those who have fought in battles since Ohio became a state in 1803.

This is a story of a hidden gem—a best-kept secret that wants to shout: "They are here! Come and honor them—those who sacrificed."

Foreword

I'm Bob McCullough, a Korean Defense veteran (1969–1970) and a Vietnam War veteran (1970–1971). In 2022 I was asked to join the board of trustees at the Ohio Veterans Memorial Park (OVMP) after I worked to get over $60,000 in donations to get the 1,822 Korean War veterans' names from Ohio engraved on the longest freestanding memorial wall in the country. At the beginning of 2024, there were projects we wanted to complete but required funding, so I attended a few grant-writing classes at the Akron Public Library. After completing a few classes I told the OVMP trustees at a monthly meeting about the writing classes and asked if anyone would be interested in helping me with writing grants. Erin Rader, a new member on the OVMP Board of Trustees, stated that not only was she a registered nurse practitioner but her last assignment at MetroHealth Hospital was writing grants for the hospital. I was ecstatic to find an experienced person who was a perfect match for the job. We initially met at my house to work on the four Seals of Transparency we would need to apply for grants. We received our Bronze, Silver, and Gold Seals, but while working on our Platinum Seal, Erin heard all the stories about getting OVMP to where it is today. And here we are! 2025 would be the twentieth anniversary of the inception of the park.

We validated her idea to write the story of the park by meeting with numerous individuals who were directly involved with OVMP from the beginning to determine if it would make interesting reading. As we interviewed an individual, they would tell us about another individual we should interview. Erin would go off searching through websites and writing letters to verify she had located the correct person, then she would set up a date to interview that person. I would go with her to the interviews to make sure we didn't miss anything, but she was the driving force. She wanted to make sure what she wrote about OVMP was as accurate as possible and more than just one side of the story, whether or not it was good or bad. She really went out of her way and worked very hard at researching all the information told to us during the interviews to make sure it was correct.

The book about OVMP starts before the site was even established. The site was originally going to be in the Mansfield area in 2005, but that changed due to a lot of differences, politics, and many, many discussions in the Mansfield area. It fell through. But the dream of having a memorial park for Ohio veterans wasn't going to stop in Mansfield. Some of the individuals from the Akron area, who were involved with the Mansfield location, took it upon themselves to find a site in the Akron area of Summit County. Once again, through hard work and with the determination to get a veteran memorial built, they found a place in Clinton, Ohio, that worked well for everyone involved.

The reader will find that Erin is a talented writer, describing all the highs and lows, the positives and negatives, that it took to build this beautiful veterans' memorial park in Clinton, Ohio. It is a place that honors these veterans who gave their all and sacrificed everything for the freedom we enjoy today. I'm sure there are stories you will read that bring joy, as well as some that will bring tears. I would like to congratulate Erin on her fortitude and driving force to get this book completed in such a short time period. Erin wrote this book while caring for her dying husband, Duke. He passed on October 31, 2024. She finished

Foreword

her last chapter with Duke, the same day she finished the last chapter of the book.

Thank you, Erin!

Bob McCullough

OVMP Trustee

Vietnam Veteran of America, Chapter 717

Korean War Defense Veteran, Chapter 138

Preface

"Waterfall above the POW pond-photo credit Steve Wallis"

Erin: (gazing across the park at dusk)
"No one could have known this park would turn out to be this beautiful."
Ken: (sharing the view)
"I did."

Imagine a place where time stands still, where every corner holds a quiet fascination, and where the bustle of everyday life fades away—a sanctuary for the soul, where the magic of nature blends seamlessly with solace. The memorials, nestled among the emerald grass, offer a connection to the past. Their strength and permanence stand unyielding, symbols of resilience. You feel it too; maybe you can endure, just as they have.

In the distance, water flows, not with the roar of a waterfall, but with a soft, musical hum. At the heart of this tranquil place stands a long black wall, towering and reflective, mirroring the blue sky. You place your hand on its smooth, cool surface, and as you breathe deeply, the moment feels profound, emotional. It embodies mortality, remembrance, and respect. You exhale. This is a place of healing, of enduring memories, of legacies left behind—a lasting presence that reaches into the future. This is our park, the Ohio Veterans Memorial Park.

When I began volunteering at the park, I quickly realized how differently military veterans see the world. Compared to me, their perspective was striking: I want to clean up the roses wilting on the granite benches. "No," they say, "let the visitors see them, let them linger a few more days." I want to wash the dirt crusted on the sticks holding the small American flags donated from cemeteries for school children. "No," they say, "this dirt comes from the soldiers' graves the flags were taken from."

Families are invited by Ken to witness the engraving of their sons' and daughters' names into the granite, a poignant tribute to their ultimate sacrifice. It's a gesture I wouldn't have thought to consider.

With reverence, Ken explains, "Look down from this view up here. You can see the tank, the helicopter. They're guarding the park, guarding our soldiers on the wall. Everything has meaning here."

The veterans and volunteers come to the park early in the morning, and they're there at night. They arrive quietly, tending to small tasks. They bend down to pluck a lone weed from the brick walkway, sensing when to approach a visitor and when to leave them to their thoughts. This place is very special to them.

I began to see how deeply their priorities were grounded in devotion to country, service, and sacrifice—a mindset that stands apart from the general focus on personal everyday needs. Something about this park draws these volunteers, holds them, even obsesses them.

I became hooked myself. At first, it was the serenity and peace of the quiet hours at dusk, as I carefully maneuvered hoses, avoiding coins and tokens left for never-forgotten soldiers while watering flowers around the monuments. Then I became hooked on their stories, connecting the emotions, values, and shared experiences of wartime and grief to this landscape.

The stories transported me, offering a view of the world I had never known. This park, this narrative, much of it provided by Ken, and the lives of the servicemen, women, and their families, all reflect the complex journeys of life. These stories open minds and change hearts, challenging beliefs and igniting the imagination. How do we capture this human experience, to connect with each other and find meaning in the unimaginable tragedies engraved in the names on the wall, on the monuments? We can try. . .

The 3095

Walk slowly past these names inscribed
"Count three thousand ninety-five"
See the face of freedom's cost
The many acts of valor and pride
The soldier's patriotic path
That they did not survive

These men and women proudly served
Left friends and family far behind
To face an unfamiliar land
Filled with death and battle lines

And where each soldier finally fell
There flowed a blood-red sign
That duty and courage walked here once
In that distant, brutal time

God then gathered each precious soul
Upon this hallowed granite wall
Called our Ohio heroes home
"Count three thousand ninety-five"
Forever healed and not alone
And safely back on heaven's side

Preface

With fingertips and tears we touch
The harsh reality of war
Victory's gain demands our loss
Of a loved one home no more

Lest we forget, our soldiers had
Hopes and dreams and future plans
Their sacrifice surrendered
Now all they ask of you and me
Walk slowly past these names inscribed
"Count three thousand ninety-five"
And with grateful hearts . . . remember!

—Kay McNaul

Engraved on the Ohio Vietnam Veterans' Memorial Wall

CHAPTER ONE

In peace children inter their parents, war violates the order of nature and causes parents to inter their children.

—Herodotus, *Histories*

1966, 2004–2006

The green car with Army insignia arrived at Adela's mother's home. Inside the house, Adela was with her children: Ann Frances (3), Jesse Ray (2), and Virginia (just two months old). Adela's mother was standing inside the screen door when the officers approached. Adela came up behind her.

"I remember going through the door to get away from what they were trying to tell me. That Jesse had been killed in his helicopter in Vietnam." Adela recalled. "I ran down the street screaming. My brother William then came to collect me from the middle of the road." She had become a widow with three small children; the love of her life was gone.

Premonitions still haunt Adela to this day: "I told Jesse I was going to marry him long before we even started dating," she recalled. "And that last time at the airport, I told him I knew it would be the last time I would see him. I left the house that day, before the officers came, and went to my mother's, not even knowing how to drive the new car he bought me. I was so unsettled—I just needed to be with my family. I left in such a hurry that I didn't even lock the house."

Adela is a Christian and believes she will see Jesse again. She still dreams of him, but in those dreams, he is always walking away from her. She carries a sense of guilt for surviving without him. "I still love him, and I often wonder what he would look like at eighty-four years old. If he had lived, I know my life would have been completely different."

"Warrant Officer Jesus Delarosa, Jr., 119th Assault Helicopter Company-courtesy of Delarosa family"

Warrant Officer (W-2) Jesús Delarosa Jr. died on July 19, 1966, just twenty-seven days after arriving in Vietnam. The helicopter he piloted collided with another aircraft, and he, along with several soldiers,

Chapter One

did not survive. For decades, Adela knew little more than this. The story was another tragic episode—a family irrevocably changed by the horror of war. As painful as the details of a death may be, loved ones often seek to understand what happened, hoping to know what their family members endured in those final moments.

"No, I don't want a ride back now. I'm going to stay here and clean up like I was told to do!" said Lieutenant Thomas Jones of the 25th Infantry to Captain Johnson. He ducked beneath the blades of the helicopter, ready to continue tagging enemy equipment at the devastated site where the 1st Battalion, 14th Infantry, of the 25th Infantry Taskforce had mortared the Viet Cong (VC) just hours earlier. The UH-1 Huey helicopter of the Assault Helicopter Combat Unit lifted off, carrying confiscated weapons and materials, and headed back to the 119th Aviation Group Station at Camp Holloway near Pleiku. On board were six soldiers, including the pilot Jesús Delarosa Jr.

Suddenly, Lieutenant Jones heard a deafening explosion. He looked up to see a chaotic swirl of metal and debris. About a mile away, at 1,500 feet, an L-19 reconnaissance plane— a spotter commonly known as a "Bird Dog"—had collided with the helicopter. The plane's pilot had not seen the Huey in his path, and the helicopter had not spotted the plane approaching from behind. The collision was catastrophic; the plane's wing sheared off the rotor blade of the helicopter, sending both aircraft crashing to the ground.

"It fell like rocks," Jones recalled later. Most likely, neither the plane's pilot nor the men in the Huey understood what had happened when they collided. The helicopter's shattered metal fragments, along with what remained of the crew, tumbled and spun, engulfed in flames as they plummeted to the ground. The plane, left with only one wing, spiraled into the Ia Drang River below.

Jones knew there would be no survivors, including his fellow soldiers from the 25th Infantry. He was in shock, overwhelmed by grief, and it took him a few moments to realize that he had narrowly missed what would have been a ride to his own death. Nightmares from that day would haunt him for decades.

Those who later assessed the situation believed that Jesse and his crew had risen from a deep jungle clearing, a gap in the canopy blasted open by artillery the night before. They might have been focused on monitoring the mortar fire to their east. Meanwhile, the fixed-wing plane's pilot Captain Charles Getman was likely scanning for enemy targets to the west, toward the Cambodian border.

The helicopter, piloted by Jesse Delarosa, carried a crew of three, Johnny E. Long (copilot), James M. Radselovage (gunner and crew chief), and Leroy Barnes—along with two passengers, Captain Raymond E. Johnson and First Sergeant Yoshiiwa Nagato of the 14th Infantry. They had taken off earlier than planned for a trash-pickup mission and an evening flight to adjust mortar and artillery fire around their defensive perimeter at Camp Holloway. All six men perished, along with Captain Getman, the pilot of the plane. The day after the crash, the 25th Infantry braved a monsoon to recover the remains of these men.

Jesse had a younger brother who was in elementary school when the helicopter went down. Several decades later, this brother, Dan Delarosa now living in Ohio, would plan to honor his brother. He sought to memorialize Jesse, a Texan, and those who died with him along with all Ohioans who died in the Vietnam War by erecting a monument, a wall with names of the Ohio dead and a helicopter, displayed in the air.

In 2005, the small group he pulled together, now calling themselves a committee, sought out a memorial builder. They found Kenneth Noon, a co-owner of Summit Memorials in Akron, Ohio. Ken, an

Chapter One

Army veteran who was too young to have served in Vietnam, recalled how they discovered him. "They told me they found me by visiting the Ohio Western Reserve National Cemetery," he said. This 274-acre veterans' cemetery, which opened in 2000, is about twenty-five miles from Akron, Ohio.

"Someone mentioned that they had walked around the cemetery, looking at gravestones that stood out to them. After researching who made the monuments they liked, Dan reached out to me at my business."

Ken was immediately interested. "It was a big job, and it honored veterans. I loved that. It would be a challenge, but I hoped I'd be the one to take it on." At that point, he was not asked to build the monuments yet, but the committee did have two requests. "They wanted me to calculate how long the wall would need to be to fit 3,095 names on it. They also asked me to attend their meetings, which were scattered across the Mansfield area. I said yes to both. I figured the wall would be an imposing 125 feet long and six to seven feet tall."

They carried the park model everywhere. They went to VFW posts, county fairs, a traveling Vietnam wall exhibit, festivals—anywhere they could build interest. Soon, they had a solid team, several of whom were veterans, and they began searching for land in Richland County.

One key encounter was with Delmer Milhoan, who met Dan and saw the model at a traveling Vietnam wall event in Barberton, Ohio, in 2005. Delmer is an Army veteran who served in Vietnam and Cambodia and holds two Purple Hearts and a Bronze Star. He had volunteered for guard duty at the event and met Ken for the first time. "I was in," Delmer said. "I was totally committed to this Ohio Vietnam wall that would honor my two buddies who died in the war." At the time, the committee was considering property in Mansfield.

*"The Ohio State Reformatory, Mansfield Ohio-
courtesy of the Ohio State Reformatory"*

That location was the Ohio State Reformatory, a historic facility on the outskirts of the industrial city of Mansfield. Built after the U.S. Civil War, it was initially designed to imprison and rehabilitate men. The imposing architecture, a blend of styles, is reminiscent of another era. The grounds feature a large pond and a long tree-lined drive to the main entrance. The site also gained fame as a filming location for the 1994 film *The Shawshank Redemption.* Now a museum, the reformatory offers tours of the historic prison, including the six-story blocks of cramped cells that once held three times more prisoners than they were designed for before it was closed in 1990.

The pond appealed to Dan, who envisioned not only a Vietnam memorial wall but also a body of water to display a Huey helicopter—the pinnacle of his tribute to Jesse. He wanted to stage the helicopter as though it had crashed into the water or as if it were rescuing a soldier from the water.

Larry Corn joined the committee in early 2005. A Marine Vietnam War veteran, he was now a veteran services officer at the Richland

Chapter One

County Veterans Service Commission and lived near Dan in Bellville. "I saw a pamphlet about a group looking to build a Vietnam memorial wall in Ohio. As a Vietnam vet, I thought it was a great idea and got involved early on."

Larry quickly recognized the group's need for guidance. They were collecting donations with no understanding of how to run a nonprofit organization. He offered his advice on starting a 501(c)(3) and provided his lawyer's contact information to assist with the application process.

In September 2005, Dan and his family, who were core members of the committee, began the process of forming the Ohio Vietnam Veterans Memorial Park (OVVMP) as a 501(c)(3) nonprofit organization. The application process could take a year or more, requiring details about the property and a builder's commitment to the project. Ken Noon of Summit Memorials, who had been an eager visitor to the group's meetings, was asked to provide a brief bid for the future job.

The 501(c)(3) application began in November 2005. Under Exhibit A, Dan had explicitly written: "Summit Memorials is the independent contractor hired to construct the granite monument and wall that will be placed in the war memorial park. The qualifications of Summit Memorials is that it's a business of constructing granite monuments." Delarosa claimed in the application to have received estimates from different contractors and Summit Memorials was "the lowest bid received" and that the estimate was attached to Exhibit A.

In February 2006, Dan asked Ken to submit a contract for the 501(c)(3) application. Ken quickly obliged, creating the document with help from his secretaries Barb Freeman and Deb Rorrer. "We received a signed copy back at the office later," Deb recalled. Ken's original estimate hadn't been sufficient for those processing the application, so he prepared a formal contract specifying that the offer was valid for ninety days. This was the first contract. Within a month of submitting it, the OVVMP's tax-exempt status was granted in March 2006, allowing them to collect tax-free donations.

As the committee worked on bylaws and maintenance plans, they focused on property at the Ohio State Reformatory. Dan envisioned placing the curved wall of names by the lake, with a Huey helicopter staged. The park would also feature a Cobra helicopter and a jeep. The reformatory began negotiations with the OVVMP, discussing a land lease of one and a half acres near the lake for one dollar per year. However, parking for visitors remained a challenge, and the committee planned to seek a building grant.

Larry Corn attended a conference in Cleveland where he met Ralph Phillips, an industrialist from Shelby, Ohio, and a fellow Vietnam veteran. Phillips, a Purple Heart recipient, was interested in the Vietnam Wall project. Seeing the group struggle to find consistent meeting space in the Mansfield area, he offered one of his large homes as a gathering place.

"Phillips loved the idea of the wall and a veterans' park for Richland County," Larry recalled. "But he was clear—if he was going to invest, he wanted a say in decisions." Phillips provided $5,000 in seed money and encouraged veterans' groups, such as Amvets and Rolling Thunder, to get involved. Dan and Phillips also planned meetings with state representatives who were veterans, hoping to resolve the parking issue and secure state funding. A state representative suggested an alternative location adjacent to the reformatory, which ultimately led to disagreements about the wall's future placement.

It was a busy summer, and Dan was optimistic that they could break ground by spring 2006. But then, as often happens, unexpected events threw everything off course.

CHAPTER ONE

In November 2005, Dan attended a contentious meeting with the reformatory board, accompanied by Ralph Phillips according to Dan. "No one on their board was a veteran," Dan recalled. "One older gentleman made it clear that while they appreciated our efforts, 'that wall' wasn't going to block their beautiful pond. The way he said 'that wall' enraged me. Those young men died for our freedoms, for him. I couldn't see moving forward with people who didn't respect that." Dan decided to pull out of negotiations the next day.

Larry Corn did not remember the issue the same way. He stated Phillips also withdrew from the project but because of Dan's decisions. "I was really upset," Larry said. "Phillips could have funded the whole thing. But everyone was stuck in their own views, and I couldn't change minds."

"Ralph Phillips and Dan Delarosa with the first model of the park created for the Reformatory property- the Mansfield News Journal, 8/21/05."

The choice of the reformatory grounds had sparked another issue—this time, among Vietnam veterans themselves. When they returned home from Southeast Asia, they were not greeted as heroes.

They considered themselves lucky if family and friends met them at the airport. There were no bands, no flags—only disdain.

"Unpopular?! Hell, we were called 'baby killers'!" one veteran exclaimed. "We were spat on, booed if we wore our uniforms. I hid out for years, never talked about any of it."

"You were no more a baby killer than I was," a Vietnam veteran's grandfather, who had been celebrated as a hero after World War II, explained. "The difference was, you had newspapers and TV constantly showing the brutality of war. That's what changed things."

Even thirty years later, the wounds were still raw. The idea of placing the memorial on prison grounds felt offensive to them, evoking a sense of shame instead of honor. Without meaning to, Dan had alienated the veterans.

The reformatory plan was abandoned.

Still hopeful, Dan and his team believed 2006 would be the year they found the right property for the wall. The park committee reached out to the mayor of Mansfield and approached local manufacturers, but it was clear the memorial would not be built there.

About forty-five minutes northeast of Mansfield lies Summit County, with Akron as its county seat. Many committee members felt this was too far a distance, and some left the group. With half the organization now based in Summit County, Dan agreed it was time to explore options there.

The idea of placing the park near a freeway exit was considered for visibility, but high-cost commercial property made this difficult. Veterans' parks across the country have paid a high price for highly visible land, facing issues like vandalism, noise, and pollution.

In the early 2000s, Ohio began developing Joint Economic Development Districts, agreements between municipalities and townships to share the benefits and responsibilities of development projects. Several locations were considered by the committee, including Springfield Township and Village in Summit County, but each had its own set of complications. Through this process, the committee learned more than they expected about local governance.

They also faced a new challenge: funding a perpetual care fund. State mandated, these trusts ensure permanent maintenance for parks and cemeteries, preventing the burden from falling on local governments if the organization encounters financial trouble or goes under. Establishing such a fund could cost up to $350,000—a difficult sum to raise, especially without a built park or committed funds. It was suggested the committee allocate two dollars from every ten dollars raised to this fund.

Then, a promising opportunity arose in the southern part of Summit County in the newly formed city of New Franklin. This area was preferable to the more complex JEDD arrangements farther north. "It was still a couple of counties away from where I lived," Dan said, "and I wasn't crazy about the idea of using property there, but we were going to check it out."

New Franklin, which became a city in January 2005 through the merger of a township and village, seemed like an ideal location for the park. The potential site was once a ball field, owned by the city and next to the city hall. It included over two acres, much of it wooded with a gentle slope. Negotiations began in earnest.

Dan pointed out the advantages of the property in a local newspaper article. He liked the wooded areas, and its proximity to a police station was another plus. The mayor of New Franklin, Al Bollas, expressed pride and excitement about the possibility of hosting the Ohio Vietnam Veterans Memorial Park.

Delmer was especially fond of the property. "It had woods, and I had all these ideas of how we could show people what the jungle canopy was like. I went there walking around and daydreamed until they told me to leave," he said with a laugh.

Dan reported to the *South Side News Leader* that engineering work had begun on the New Franklin site with a groundbreaking ceremony tentatively planned for January 2007. "It feels like it's all finally coming together," he said. This was June 2006.

What was coming together was a massive project—grander than anything initially envisioned in Mansfield. With each new site the model evolved, now featuring the wall, flagpoles for each military branch and accompanying monuments, two helicopters, brick and stone paths, and numerous other monuments and benches. The committee was strong and resourceful, not so much in financial backing but in skilled and unskilled labor. They were prepared to work hard, and they would.

New Franklin appeared to be the most promising site yet. An undetermined amount of acreage was under consideration, large enough to accommodate all the components on Dan's wish list. In October 2006, the New Franklin council passed a resolution approving the project, though no lease agreement or approval by the Board of Zoning Appeals had been signed. The park committee was optimistic that this would be the location; however, a faction on the council and the law director still had concerns that needed addressing before moving forward.

One major concern was the lack of funding. There were no funds yet for perpetual care and no major donors or grantors in sight. The city's recommendation was simple: The committee needed to seek state sanctioning, which meant formally obtaining approval from the state of Ohio to build the park.

Chapter One

After researching the matter, the city council, led by the law director, believed that state sanctioning would benefit the park financially. With state approval, larger government grants and private donors might be more accessible and it would be easier to establish the perpetual care fund. The law director suggested that if the state sanctioned this memorial, they likely wouldn't authorize another Vietnam memorial elsewhere in Ohio and it would ensure the park's inclusion in state tourism literature.

But the park committee was resistant to the idea. After nearly two years of meetings between members from Akron and Mansfield, they were determined to keep the park private. They feared state involvement might lead to losing control over the project, with a risk of the park being moved to another location, such as the state capital, or the design plans being altered. They preferred to manage the project themselves, despite the fundraising challenges.

In local newspapers, Dan was quoted estimating the project's cost at $1.2 million.[1] Veterans involved at the time now say this figure was intentionally high to demonstrate the seriousness of their plans. Even at half that amount, their funding efforts seemed modest, considering the costs of building just the wall. With their tax-exempt 501(c)(3) status, they ramped up fundraising, relying on businesses, private donations, and the sale of engraved paving bricks, T-shirts, and other merchandise.

During a September 2006 committee meeting, Ken Noon was asked to become a member. He was not under any contract, as the original contract agreement from February had expired in June when the project lacked a property. Aware of potential conflicts of interest, Ken consulted his lawyer, who advised that as long as Ken didn't vote on anything related to granite contracts, he could join the committee.

In a meeting on November 21, 2006, Delmer Milhoan nominated Ken as a trustee and Dan Delarosa seconded it.

By January 2007, the New Franklin plan had fallen through and the search for a new site began. Tim Stevenhagen, a local funeral director and vice president of the park committee, was familiar with the Clinton Cemetery Association in a small village near New Franklin. Known for his pleasant demeanor and ability to mediate conflict, Tim had sensed that the New Franklin property would not work out. By late 2006, he had begun inquiring about securing a portion of the Clinton Cemetery's twelve unused acres.

The mayor of Clinton, Phyllis Mayberry, was supportive of the idea, believing the veterans' park would draw visitors to the village of 1,400 residents at that time.

The Clinton Cemetery Association was established in 1916 after about seven acres of land were donated to Clinton. Veterans from the Revolutionary War through Vietnam, as well as peacetime veterans, are buried in the Clinton Cemetery. For future use, the cemetery board purchased an additional twelve acres across the road: ten acres in 1993 and two more in 1998. This was the land Tim Stevenhagen proposed for the veterans' park, initiating negotiations with the Clinton Cemetery Board. A perpetual care fund would no longer be an issue as the cemetery had one in place.

On February 10, 2007, Dan Delarosa, park committee officer Joseph Paonessa, and the Clinton Cemetery Board reached and signed an agreement. It outlined a permanent memorial on 1.7 acres with an access road encircling it, and all responsibilities for care, maintenance, insurance, and security would fall to the veterans' organization, OVVMP. The agreement also included plans for an office building to serve both the park but would belong to the cemetery for future cemetery needs. A critical stipulation was in clause 13, which stated: "The park committee agrees to construct the memorial park in phases. No construction is to begin on any phase until all monies related to that phase have been raised, received, and collected."[2]

This provision would later play a crucial role in a conflict that threatened to bring the park committee, the cemetery board, the community, and the monument builder to their knees.

Over the years, the group behind the veterans' park evolved, with many members coming and going. Ken, who joined in 2005 and became a member in 2006, remained involved for two decades. Dan left before the groundbreaking in 2007, while Delmer, who had been with the group since 2005, decided to leave in 2008. Tim Stevenhagen remained until after the wall's dedication in 2009. Joe Paonessa held a leadership role until 2010, and Chuck Nicholas, who joined in 2008, is still on the board today.

By 2007, Larry Corn was no longer involved, but he had heard about the acquisition of the new property in Summit County. He later reflected, "I thought we should have kept it in Richland County, so it was sad for me. But honestly, it never could have become the beautiful park it is today on any property we looked at back then. It's in the perfect place."

On February 3, 2007, a crowd of about 150 gathered under a tent on the designated acreage—the future home of the Ohio Vietnam Veterans Memorial Park.

"It was frigid, and it was my wife's birthday, but she came along," Ken recalled. "We weren't going to miss this."

"It was so cold, but what an exciting day!" agreed Delmer.

This was the dedication of the land, the first of many dedications over the next nearly two decades. After a long and sometimes disheartening search, the excitement was palpable. They had finally found the place to honor the veterans who gave it all.

"Barbed wire on the Clinton property-photo credit Ken Noon"

Chapter Two

*A nation that does not honor its
heroes will not long endure.*

—Abraham Lincoln

2007–2008

How should they be remembered?

A walk through any veterans' cemetery reveals coins placed on or around gravestones—a newer tradition embraced by the veteran community as a gesture of respect since the Vietnam War. Even during times of political divide over unpopular wars, these coins serve as symbols of honor. The tradition of leaving coins dates back to ancient times when Roman soldiers placed coins in the mouths of their fallen comrades to pay the boatman for their journey to the afterlife.

Coins are scattered throughout the Ohio Veterans Memorial Park—propped along the wall, on inscribed paving bricks, at the bases of monuments, and on over one hundred memorial granite benches lining the walkways. Each denomination carries its own meaning. Pennies left near the names of veterans show respect from friends, family, acquaintances, and even strangers. Nickels are placed by soldiers who trained with the deceased. Dimes signify a deeper connection, often from soldiers who served in the same unit. But quarters are rare. When seen, they carry profound significance—left by someone who was present when the fallen soldier died, a witness to their last moments. Even heroes have heroes.

"Coins from visitors-both photos credit Steve Wallis"

This rough, uneven 1.7-acre plot would become a place where new stories of heroism would unfold. This land, and the park itself, would be dedicated to the fallen veterans, the families who sacrificed, and the builders and caretakers who honor their memory. The veterans' park committee felt the weight of this commitment. It was time to raise funds and deliver on their promise. Tim Stevenhagen and the committee were grateful the land came without governmental strings. It was private, allowing them to proceed freely, as long as they honored their agreement with the cemetery board.

The location was ideal for other reasons too. Set along a National Scenic Byway on the Ohio and Erie Canalway, where Summit, Stark, and Wayne Counties converge, it was within a mile of a state route and five miles from an interstate. It was a big idea for such a small village, but soldiers come from the towns, villages, and rural areas as well as cities and suburbs across this vast country.

Across the street from the cemetery, the memorial park was to be placed in the center of twelve acres of unused property owned by the Clinton Cemetery Association. Looking back, the association's secretary-treasurer and president, respectively, Sandra Dreurey and her husband, Edwin, were pleased they took a chance on the park committee's dream. "Edwin stepped down from the board, and I took it on," Sandra said. "It was risky, but it was the best thing we ever did for Clinton."

Edwin has since passed, and she has retired from her roles on the cemetery board, as well as her teaching and other community positions. Sandra still lives in Clinton where she was born and raised; she cherishes her hometown, which has been part of Ohio's history since 1816. Sandra has written a 179-page book, *The Clinton Story*,[1] and is working on a second volume with Amy Hilton, a fellow Clintonite and relative. It has yet to be published. Amy, now the treasurer of the Clinton Cemetery Association, shares Sandra's enthusiasm for the park: "It's just beautiful and so important to our town."

Linda Murphy, who is now president of the Clinton Cemetery board, worked for both the city and the privately owned cemetery at the time. She recalled initial concerns about the veterans' limited funds for such an ambitious project. "We had to trust them, and we knew they were determined. It was wonderful seeing what they were up to, and my husband helped at times with his company's equipment." Like Sandra, Linda was born, raised, and continues to live in Clinton. Her husband, Mike, who has since passed away, worked a crane and supported the project with the heavy lifting at the park.

Sandra's book recounts Clinton as a small village, proud of its pioneer heritage since its founding in 1816. The community celebrates every significant anniversary, and the village thrived early on because of the Ohio and Erie Canal, which ran through its center. The nearby Tuscarawas River, once powerful and abundant, provided energy and fish, while the rich soil allowed farmers to grow wheat, vegetables, and even cranberries in the swampy areas. Tall, straight trees were plentiful for lumber, and the region also saw coal mining in the following decades. The canal offered a cheaper mode of transportation than overland routes, spurring the growth of warehouses and businesses throughout the town.

However, the advent of the railroad ended the canal industry, and today, its brief but vibrant history is celebrated at annual festivals. The towpath, once used by mules to pull canalboats, has been paved and integrated into the Cuyahoga Valley National Park as part of the Ohio and Erie Canal Towpath Trail, extending beyond the park for hikers to retrace the mules' path.

Chapter Two

"Village of Clinton-photo credit Steve Wallis"

The ensemble of characters who made up the veterans' memorial park committee stood together, gazing across a fallow, sloping, weedy field—the starting point of their journey. As Joseph Campbell suggests in his philosophy of hero myths, we are all flawed characters called to adventure.[2] Among this group were Vietnam War veterans, other veterans who hadn't served in Vietnam, and nonveterans alike. All were volunteers, now facing the challenges of working together and resolving issues as they arose.

The planning became intense. A new 3D model was needed to educate potential donors. Early ideas emerged, but one thing was certain: there would be a granite wall honoring Ohioans who died in the Vietnam War and a Huey helicopter high in the air.

The newly acquired property had to be assessed, surveyed, cleaned, and leveled. Delmer and Don spent hours driving Delmer's truck across the land, dealing with various issues—including a persistent groundhog problem. "I thought I'd just blow them the hell up! That's how I used to think," Delmer recalled. Carrying a five-gallon container of gasoline, he began pouring it into one of the tunnels.

"You gonna use all that?" Don asked.

Delmer nodded. "It's what I do!" he exclaimed, and continued to pour, then tossed an M80 into the hole and the two ran to a safe distance.

Ken remembers watching as the land heaved, with puffs of smoke rising from holes across the property. "It was like a cartoon or the end of the *Caddyshack* movie. Delmer was just crazy sometimes. He was fun to watch, though," he laughed.

Despite the challenges, the project was both overwhelming and energizing. "The real work could begin," Ken said, who in his forties was the youngest of the founding members. He often took on the most physically demanding tasks. "Some of the older guys couldn't kneel or shovel for hours on end, but this was work that had to be done. We couldn't afford big machinery, so I was more than happy to take on the tougher jobs."

CHAPTER TWO

"Founders-Tim Stevenhagen, Delmer Milhoan, Kenneth Noon and Frank Sasz-OVMP archives"

There was mowing, surveying, measuring, and coordinating with contractors, many of whom generously donated materials and their crews' time. The project was coming together, but the group remained small, relying on their collective effort and determination.

One day in 2008, a motorcycle pulled up to Ken's shop, and a man in worn jeans stepped off. "I'm interested in volunteering at the veterans park," the man proclaimed. He had heard that Ken played a key role at the park and the man sought him out.

Ken asked how the man thought he could help. Ken wasn't about to turn him away, but it wasn't often that people just showed up like this. "I'm a lawyer," replied Charles Olimsky.

Ken recalled being very skeptical and responding, "No, you're not!"

But it turned out to be true. Charles was indeed an attorney, and he went on to serve on the board, volunteering his legal expertise and support in many ways. He remembers traveling for years with Ken and others, seeking donations, "trying to sell those benches," and even digging ditches for the electric lines. Charles has fond memories from those years of dedication and camaraderie.

It was clear more help was needed. A call for volunteers had gone out the previous year, and many resourceful, committed individuals responded. Among them was Joseph Paonessa, who saw the ad Tim had placed in a local paper. He lived only minutes from the property.

"I had the time and interest. I'm a veteran of the Military Police, and my brother Mike was drafted and died in Vietnam," Joe recalled. "I spent years researching the details of his death and made many friends at reunions of the 9th Infantry and D-Troop 3rd Squadron, 5th Cavalry, Mike's unit. I volunteered to work at the park in his memory."

Joe became treasurer and later president of the park committee during its early years. "I handled invoices, arranged work, and was often dragged by committee members to various locations, seeking donations and ideas for the park," he said with a laugh.

CHAPTER TWO

"PFC Michael D. Paonessa-courtesy of Paonessa family"

His brother, Michael D. Paonessa, is honored on the Ohio Vietnam Wall and has a granite bench along the brick walkway. In a bedroom at his home, Joe proudly displays Mike's medals, including a Distinguished Service Cross for extraordinary heroism. The folded triangular flag hangs in a shadow box nearby. Mike's story is a deeply personal and traumatic one that Joe cherishes, documented in a notebook filled with eyewitness accounts, an article,[3] and emails.

"I return to that war most every night," wrote Johnny Hutchinson in an email to Joe, expressing a sentiment shared by many who lived through the battle that claimed Mike's life.

In 1968, Michael was drafted into the Army. After basic training, he came home to marry, and then, in July, he was shipped out to Vietnam. He was twenty-one years old.

Stationed in the Mekong River Delta, Mike was part of the 9th Infantry, known as Doughboys. The Delta was a vast, swampy plain crisscrossed by the Mekong River and its tributaries. During the monsoon season, it became a muddy waist-deep expanse, and even in the dry season, the land barely rose above sea level. The dense jungles, reeds, and overgrown rice paddies created a challenging environment.

"Michael, one of a group in a Huey helicopter with Group 1, September, 1968-courtesy of Paonessa family"

New helicopter tactics had been developed for the region, with reconnaissance troops identifying enemy positions in flatter, drier areas. They would quickly move in and out, reporting their findings to larger infantry units who would then engage the North Vietnamese and Viet Cong (VC).

In September 1968, Mike arrived at Đồng Tâm, a U.S. division base in the Mekong, joining D-Troop, a small, tight-knit reconnaissance unit. Their mission was to locate the enemy, report back, and clear out before larger forces moved in. Essentially, they were the point men of the 9th Division's 3rd Squadron, 5th Cavalry, who had traded horses for helicopters in this war—taking on a dangerous role.

On October 18, a mission was called. Three squads, each with six troops, were dropped into a hamlet about two hundred yards from a suspected bunker system along a tree line. Earlier, a helicopter gunman had seen old men digging there, but no VC were initially believed to be present. Mike's recon group was sent to investigate, but all the villagers they questioned denied any enemy activity. Mike was tasked with manning the radio to maintain contact with support. Then, as one account put it, "all hell broke loose from the tree line." Hidden enemy forces unleashed a barrage of fire, hitting several troops.

Survivors described the chaos: "[We] could feel and hear rounds over and around us, both in the air and passing through the reeds. Thank God for the reeds, they gave us enough cover to survive," wrote Jim Flynn. Soldiers Ron Delp, John Marshall, and medic Wayne Benes were wounded, with Doc Benes shot while assisting Marshall. Following the lieutenant's order, Mike radioed for a helicopter to evacuate the injured.

Spotting the incoming helicopter, Mike climbed a rice paddy dike to signal its location. Typically, smoke would be used to mark the spot, but this time they avoided it to prevent drawing more enemy fire. Instead, Mike bravely hand-signaled the helicopter in. John Marshall was loaded aboard, and as the helicopter tried to lift off, accounts suggest that the lieutenant stood near Mike when a rocket-propelled grenade (RPG) struck the tail boom. Mike pushed the lieutenant away as the helicopter fell and rolled, pinning Mike under the right skid and fuel leaking into the swampy weeds. A helicopter weighs six thousand pounds, and Mike was trapped on the enemy side.

The lieutenant shouted for the men to clear out on the safe side of the crash, as the helicopter continued to leak fuel. Tracer rounds fired by the VC could ignite it at any moment, making the situation more perilous.

Centering behind the downed helicopter, the soldiers continued to fire into the tree line. All the men, except Mike, moved back toward the hamlet. They couldn't reach Mike trapped under the skid, and prayed he was still alive and could be rescued soon. But some later admitted they believed he was probably gone.

When the larger infantry unit arrived, they were informed about Mike's situation. Their mission was to push back the enemy, find the missing medic, and recover Mike. The remaining Doughboys and the downed helicopter crew, along with the injured John Marshall, were evacuated. Ron Delp's body was recovered, but Mike and Doc Benes were still missing. Doc's body was later found in the tree line, where he had crawled after saving Marshall's life.

The larger unit soon found themselves pinned down by mortar rounds and their supporting aircraft under fire, making it impossible to reach Mike. No one back at base knew if he was still alive or if the infantry could reach him. The following day, October 19, after the VC had withdrawn, a helicopter flew over the crash site. As it passed over the downed helicopter, the crew saw movement in the water near the skid. Someone was alive.

Michael Paonessa was barely clinging to life. For hours, he had been trapped, breathing in and swallowing JP-4, a corrosive, highly flammable jet-fuel blend. He was evacuated to the Mobile Army Surgical Hospital, or MASH, at Đồng Tâm, but on October 19, 1968, he succumbed to his chemical burns and injuries.

Months of hard work lay ahead before the groundbreaking ceremony for the wall. In 2008, Ken applied for the role of monument builder and won the bid. "Other companies estimated the project. I took the time to map it out," he said in an article in *The Suburbanite* prior to the wall's dedication in May 2009. "My wife put all the names in alphabetical order to determine the exact size of the wall. It is 125 feet long, made up of 50 panels, each 30 inches wide and 6 feet tall. Each panel weighs a ton and is 8 inches thick."[4]

Chapter Two

This design allowed the wall to stand without support, making it the longest freestanding monument in the nation at the time. Unlike the Vietnam Memorial wall in Washington, D.C., which is reinforced by a hill behind it, this wall in Ohio would stand on its own. But it would take many more months before the granite structure would rise.

The effort to sell memorial bricks felt endless. Thousands needed to be sold to raise the necessary funds. Volunteers attended every event, festival, and crowded mall they could think of to promote the bricks. One day, they encountered a Vietnam veteran who was upset about having to pay for a brick. He did not feel he should have to pay. "I'm a Vietnam vet, and so were my friends. Why don't I just get a brick with my name in this park?" he asked angrily. Explanations did not satisfy him. At home that evening, his wife explained to him that the bricks were for any serviceperson's name and the money paid for the wall that would honor fallen veterans; he cooled off, returned the next day, and purchased four—three for his friends and one for himself.

"Delmer using a Bobcat to dig postholes for the wooden wall-OVMP archives"

To represent the wall's significance, the committee built a wooden replica at the exact position and length where the granite would stand on the field. It served as a visual symbol for visitors and potential donors. Posts were erected, and eight-by-four-foot plywood sheets were nailed lengthwise, forming a 125-foot structure. It was painted black with white lattice fencing from its bottom edge to the ground. This imposing wooden wall became a striking focal point for the groundbreaking ceremony.

A young man visiting the park asked if he could write on the black wooden wall. He had lost a friend in Vietnam and wanted to honor him on this symbolic structure. Permission was granted, and soon a trend began. Committee members put out buckets of markers, and before long, the wall was covered with sentiments. Names and ranks were scrawled alongside messages like "Uncle," "Grandpa," and "Dad." Epitaphs read "My son, I'll miss you forever," "They were good people," and a simple peace symbol with the word "Now." Bouquets and ribbons were attached to the lattice below.

"It was a shame to take down the wall and burn it later," Ken said. "We had nowhere to store it, but people had become quite attached to it. It meant a lot to some folks." This was more than sentimentality—the wall had already begun to serve as an instrument of healing.

"A visitor writing a heartfelt message on the wooden wall-OVMP archives"

Dan Czartoszewski and his younger brother Bryon wrote their names and epitaphs to loved ones on the wooden wall. Dan had dug the holes for the posts that held it up. His mother, Linda, was one of the individuals who would break ground with a golden shovel. She was a staunch park supporter and volunteer for several years. Her husband was a Vietnam veteran, drafted into the Army. During his deployment, Henry "Hank" Czartoszewski, SP4, E4, was able to come home on a "compassionate leave" through the Red Cross who facilitated the process, ensuring he got home to address the matter of his newborn son, Dan's older brother Henry Jr., who was having difficulties. While Hank was home, where he'd been stationed in Vietnam was bombed, and he didn't return. He spent the last twenty years of his life battling cancer and other illnesses caused by exposure to Agent Orange. "Dad never talked about Vietnam until the last years of his life," Dan recalled. "He loved the idea of the veterans' memorial park, but he was unable to work there himself." Hank's was the first bench to be dedicated in the park.

Dan, however, spent years contributing to the park with equipment from his company, Daniels, Inc. From the wooden wall to the footers for the granite wall, from the trenches for electrical work to the POW/MIA pond, he was deeply involved in preparing the grounds. His brother Bryon also made significant contributions by helping Dan and ensuring the heating and air conditioning work for the Family of Heroes Hall.

Ken fondly recalled Dan's contributions, not just the hard work but also the great food he prepared. "We couldn't have done it without that kind of help. But the meals he cooked, especially the steaks he grilled, were something else!"

Dan admitted modestly that cooking was just another way to give. His wife, Kathi, worked behind the scenes, helping Dan and her father. It was truly a family affair, with her father, Dick Elvin, also contributing as a longtime committee member and volunteer. U.S. Army Second Lieutenant Richard E. Elvin served as the company commander of the 378th at Fort Irwin, California, from 1963–1965. He would be a speaker at the groundbreaking event to come, and a bench has been dedicated in his honor, commemorating his service to the park and his country.

The plans for the park's groundbreaking were complicated but exciting. Committee meetings were lengthy, each member deeply involved in setting up the event. During this time, there were a few disagreements. Dan Delarosa was still running the meetings, in Clinton or the Mansfield area, but his involvement was becoming strained.

One major challenge was finding a Huey helicopter. The model was still in use, and old ones were needed for parts. Dan searched everywhere, from private owners to political channels, even reaching out to the White House while inviting President Bush to the groundbreaking. He received a polite, noncommittal response from the president's staff.

"My health wasn't great, and it was wearing on me that the park was so far from where I originally wanted it placed," Dan said. He eventually resigned from the committee before the groundbreaking.

Many military groups were notified about the groundbreaking event. This park had been a long time coming for Vietnam veterans, and many wanted to be involved from the start. Many groups expressed interest: the Gold Star Mothers, VFWs, and American Legion posts. The committee planned flyovers.

On August 25, 2007, historical and educational war re-enactors Marlboro Volunteers, Inc., arrived early, setting up military displays and two cannons from the 19th Ohio Light Artillery Infantry on the surrounding lawns. Hundreds of veterans, families, friends, and local residents gathered to mark the occasion. Seven color guard groups were present, bagpipes from the College of Wooster played, and cannons fired, startling children and adults alike. Representatives from nearby cities and counties, and even state officials, attended. Among the crowd was Dan, who had driven up from Mansfield. He brought a picture of his brother Jesse. He'd been asked to break ground with one of the golden shovels.

"Civil War reenactors in the Marlboro Volunteers, Inc.-OVMP archives"

Tons of crushed limestone had been laid down to replace mulch in flag-lined pathways, forming the base for thousands of bricks to come. The phrase "Lest We Forget," planned for the granite wall, was prominently displayed on the black wooden wall in golden vinyl letters, becoming a focal point for the gathering. Clinton's Mayor Phyllis Mayberry, the second most-decorated Vietnam veteran Col. Dennis Tomcik, local celebrity Dick Goddard, and news anchor Eric Mansfield were present. Goddard sang the national anthem, and the nine honorees

Chapter Two

stepped forward to take hold of golden shovels. Cheers erupted as the proclamation was made—the ground was officially broken, and the building of the Ohio Vietnam Veterans Memorial Park had begun. A 21-gun salute followed, and twenty-one white doves were released. The digging to start the concrete foundation commenced that afternoon.

Tim, now the group's vice-president and spokesperson for the day, said, "The memorial is more than a list of names. We want to be a place where memories and healing can come. It will remind us of the high cost of our freedoms. . . . They are not dead so long as we remember them."[5]

The excitement was punctuated by more cannon fire, then a solemn stillness as U.S. Army Sergeant First Class Larry Smith raised his trumpet and sounded "Taps."

"Beginning of the services at the groundbreaking-OVMP achives"

"I painted those shovels gold for the groundbreaking," Ken recalled . Two of them, now with the gold nearly worn away, were recently found in a storage area that hadn't been accessed for a decade. To the delight of Tim's brother and daily volunteer John Stevenhagen, the 2007 3D model of the park was also recovered from the damp space. John, who devotes his time to park maintenance, had never seen it before.

"I can't believe it's still intact!" John exclaimed as he cleaned the model. He hopes to create a museum and archive of the park's history with this model as a centerpiece. Ken, who designed it, said, "It's been through a lot. We took it everywhere to raise funds." Chuck Nicholas, a veteran and longtime board member, was the only other person who had seen the model years before.

Chuck has been involved with the committee "before it was called a board" since 2008, serving as president multiple times. "I had health issues and would step down, then step back up when needed," he said.

Chuck, a Navy Vietnam War veteran, was known as a "River Rat." He served on patrol boats, fighting up and down the Mekong River and its tributaries as part of the Brown Water Navy. In 1964–1965, his boat was assigned to peacekeeping and was to be nonaggressive. But with the introduction of Operation Market Time, their mission shifted to locating, tracking, and stopping vessels along the coast—tasked with capturing or destroying any that posed a threat.[6]

Chuck served with Task Force 115, operating like a game warden searching for contraband. "We mostly inspected sampans and junks," he recalled. Their mission was to "search and seize" while patrolling coastal waters and rivers. Eight men were stationed on his boat, a Monitor—a highly modified version of the LCM-6, a mobile riverine assault boat with a powerful Cummins diesel engine that could reach twelve knots. "That's really fast on a river," Chuck explained. Most of the crew were

Chapter Two

Navy petty officers with one or two Army personnel and always a Vietnamese national who could interpret.

The boat was heavily armed. Each crew member carried 1911s and M16s, along with a 40 mm cannon, two double-barreled .50-caliber machine guns (Chuck manned one of these), and a .30-caliber gun. If that wasn't enough, they had an M80 rocket launcher and a flamethrower, known as a Zippo. Still, none of this could protect them from river mines, so a Coast Guard escort or other military boats with minesweepers always led the way searching for underwater explosives. It was unnerving to search the sampans, never knowing what they might uncover. "They'd be piled six feet high with rice, and a skinny guy would be pushing the boat upriver with a tiny engine and a long stick. We'd have to stop him and shove our rifles into the rice piles. One time, we found boxes of AK-47s meant for the VC. We had to take the guy to the barge and turn him in."

"The Monitor, boat of Chuck Nicholas and crew, on the Mekong River-courtesy of Chuck Nicholas"

Chuck remembered a fellow sailor, Ernie Johnson, a boatswain's mate third class, or BM3, who served as the loader for Chuck's gun. "He kept talking about wanting to go home. He made the mistake of standing up and was killed by gunfire from the trees," Chuck said sadly. It was the only fatality on their boat during his deployment.

The trees along the shore were always the most frightening, especially during night patrols. "We ran dark, but our boat was loud—a diesel. We looked for lit cigarettes, smoke, or any kind of light, constantly scanning the shore. It was scary," he recalled.

Chuck served in Vietnam for nine months and twenty-one days, and he didn't escape without injury. "I got speared in the right shoulder. I stupidly stood up from my protective steel barrier around my gun. I've had two surgeries on that over the years."

River Rats were some of the fiercest warriors, disrupting enemy traffic and securing the rivers. They lost boats to mines, and RPGs could blast through twelve inches of conventional steel. "If you had to get out of the boat—and you tried never to do that—the mud was up to your knees. The river was wide, brown, and moved fast."

"We hated seeing the kids try to swim out to the boat," he recalled "The Mekong River is awful—nothing living should be in it. So we'd go close to shore and throw them candy, gum, and coins. They were cute, those poor kids. That was one of the nicest things for us—those kids."

The preservation of stories—like those of Jesse, Mike, and Chuck—is essential for future generations to understand the impact of war. Recognize and remember. Listen and remember. Write it down and remember. Lest we forget.

CHAPTER THREE

We choose to believe that granite is alive. If life is movement, then rock—with its atoms flying around like stars in cosmos—is alive.

—Yvon Chouinardt, *Let My People Go Surfing*

2009

The Ohio Vietnam wall is built of black granite from India, similar to the Vietnam Memorial in Washington, D.C. Polished to a mirror-like finish, the surface is smooth, cool, and reflective, embodying both strength and elegance. Granite, the second hardest natural stone after diamond, replaced marble for monuments in the late nineteenth century due to its durability. When granite is carved, the crystals that make up the rock shatter. Shaping granite requires specialized tools and produces harmful silica dust, making early monuments costly and exclusive until industrial ventilation was introduced in the 1930s.[1]

One of granite's key properties is its durability, allowing it to endure weathering and erosion while maintaining its natural beauty. From the start, the wall was spoken of by committee members as if it were a character—resilient, defiant, and capable of conveying strength. Beyond its presence, the wall was envisioned as a vessel for emotions and memories. It would transcend its physical role, offering a space for reflection and healing.

"Visitors remembering their loved ones-photo credit Steve Wallis"

As the land was prepared, the 3,095 names of Ohioans killed in action (KIA) in the Vietnam War were gathered from Washington, D.C. The names represent soldiers from the Army, Marines, Air Force, Navy, and Coast Guard, with only one being female, an Army nurse. The term *soldier* in this narrative is used broadly to include those in the named military branches as well as the National Guard, the Merchant Marine, and all other military groups.

Occasionally, visitors were disappointed to find a loved one's name missing. This was because names were determined by the soldier's "home of record"—the state where they enlisted, were drafted, or began active duty. If an Ohioan enlisted in another state, like Michigan, their name would not appear on the Ohio wall.

In June 2008, the committee president, Joe Paonessa signed the contract with Summit Memorials Inc. The plan and the cost remained the same as the first contract that had expired in 2006. The committee also learned that for future bids, factors beyond cost, such as financing, could be considered. Ken ended up financing the wall by accepting payments later on. Though he stayed on the board, he followed his lawyer's advice and refrained from voting on anything related to the granite, payments, or financial decisions. "I really stayed away from that financial end of things," he recalled.

Throughout 2008, a surge of fundraising activities took place: motorcycle poker runs, raffles, parades, and festivals, all featuring donation boxes along with hats, T-shirts, and engraved paving bricks for sale. The park's first website launched, allowing online donations via PayPal. The committee also visited local city councils, asking for donations or encouraging communities to show their support by purchasing bricks, memorial stones, and benches.

The idea of memorial granite benches along the park walkways served both a functional and fundraising purpose. Benches, traditionally for rest and reflection, would be black granite to match the wall and cost $3,500 each. Summit Memorials' cost to the park was $1,200 per bench, with an additional $500 to cover design, etching, and placement. The remaining $1,800 contributed to park funds, a financial structure that remains unchanged. Due to space limitations, a set number of benches were planned, along with sales of bricks, individual monuments, and tiles—fundraising strategies that still maintain their original prices over fifteen years later.

"Bench dedication-OVMP archives"

The committee began by approaching nearby communities to sell benches inscribed with the names of cities or towns, reflecting their support for veterans. Their efforts expanded across northeastern Ohio and beyond, believing that communities would be proud to honor their fallen. Many responded, and more than thirty benches were ordered before the wall's dedication. Today, over one hundred benches line the walkways, a testament to the ongoing support for the park.

In early 2007, Chelle Rossi, president of the Clinton Historical Society, joined the park committee. She was very active in the local communities and highly recommended for the committee by the Clinton Cemetery Board. She initially attended meetings as a visitor before becoming a key member. Chelle quickly took charge of fundraising, successfully reaching out to foundations and corporations.

"She was so good at it," Joe recalled, who was president-treasurer of the park committee at the time. "Soon she became vice-president, and she teamed up with me as we scheduled numerous excursions to groups in various communities, VFWs, and other organizations to discuss the needs of the park."

Several past board members remembered participating in presentations, both small and large, to promote the park. They collectively recalled it as a busy and exciting time, with benches and monuments being sold.

Even the physical work on the site was enjoyable. Volunteers spent long days at the park, ordering pizza; other times, wives and friends brought sandwiches. The grass was regularly mowed by alternating volunteers, and local companies loaned equipment.

The land, which sloped to the right when viewed from the road, needed leveling. Schalmo Homes, a local construction company, donated over one hundred truckloads of fill dirt from basements dug for new homes. "Can you imagine how much that would have cost?" said Ken. But the volunteers still had to move the dirt.

By this time, the park committee had raised about $40,000, with anticipated additional grants and pledged donations. Ken was thrilled to finally have the granite contract in hand and the property ready for construction.

"The guy I ordered the Indian black granite from was eager to handle this project. He knew how committed the park committee was. But we didn't have the full payment. Nowhere near," Ken said.

The granite supplier agreed to order the fifty panels needed and gave the park a year from the time the granite arrived in the U.S. to complete the payment. The park committee accepted, and the granite was ordered, with the wall dedication planned for Memorial Day 2009, the following year.

The massive shipment of black granite arrived from India at Summit Memorials just before Thanksgiving 2008, and the engravers began their solemn work of inscribing thousands of names.

"Getting the names of the Vietnam fallen on the wall at Summit Memorial shop-photo credit Ken Noon"

The other side of the wall, a broad black expanse, was designed to depict the history of U.S. wars since Ohio became a state in 1803, from the War of 1812 to the wars with Iraq and Afghanistan. Fifteen panels at the south end were left blank, reserved for the names of Korean War KIAs, a future project requiring additional funding. The very early historical narratives of these conflicts are portrayed on the Ohio Vietnam Memorial Wall, acknowledging Ohio's role and honoring those who served.

CHAPTER THREE

The numbers of the U.S. dead are sobering reminders that, even centuries later, the fallen should continue to be remembered. The War of 1812 was the first conflict fought after Ohio achieved statehood. Between 15,000 and 20,000 U.S. soldiers died, both from combat and disease. In the Mexican-American War (1846–1848), about 13,000 Americans died. The American Civil War (1861–1865) had a combined death toll of approximately 850,000 military casualties from both the North and South. The Spanish-American War (April 21–August 13, 1898) claimed 2,446 American lives.[2]

"Representations of past conflicts on the granite wall-OVMP archives"

"Etching of the Mexican War on the granite wall-OVMP archives"

Memorial Day, originally created to honor Civil War soldiers, has since evolved to include all conflicts. The names of soldiers from more recent conflicts were added north of the historical panels. These were inscribed before the names from the Korean War because families of soldiers killed in the War on Terrorism were able to fund the inclusion of their loved ones. Fewer family members remained to honor those who died in Korea, necessitating a different funding approach.

In January 2009, Chelle Rossi visited Ken's studio at Summit Memorials. Skilled workers were busy with their usual tasks, fashioning gravestones and, more significantly, etching the names into the memorial wall's fifty granite panels. During a meeting with the *Akron Beacon*

CHAPTER THREE

Journal, Rossi expressed how thrilling it was to witness the work being done in the shop. "I'm confident that once people see what a wonderful memorial it is, we'll have no trouble raising the rest of the money." She stated that people "will fall in love" with the park. The article featured a photo of Ken carving the *Gold Star Mother* statue with a pneumatic chisel. A Gold Star mother is a mother who has lost a child who was a military serviceman or servicewoman while serving in action. It extends to the father (a Gold Star father) and to the family as well (a Gold Star family).[3]

A favorable month of weather in March 2009 allowed Ken to bring the granite panels to the park, enabling the wall to be completed on schedule if the weather continued to cooperate. The plan called for each black granite panel to be six feet tall, thirty inches wide, and eight inches thick, each panel weighing nearly a ton. Proper handling and teamwork were crucial as Ken and his crew dealt with the heavy materials, using a combination of cranes and manpower.

"Volunteer, Dennis Antal, working on the base of the wall, the original barn in the background-OVMP archives"

The wall was designed to be freestanding, so structural stability was key. Alignment and leveling were vital as Ken meticulously sealed the stone pieces together to form one continuous 125-foot wall, especially given the wind that often swept across the open field from the west. Fortunately, the mild weather continued, allowing work to proceed smoothly.

Above the names on the west side of the wall, at the center of the memorial, are the words "Lest We Forget." This phrase, which evolved from literary origins to honor fallen soldiers, is a poignant expression of collective memory and respect.[4] Although no one could recall exactly when the decision was made to use this phrase, it stands out in large gold-leafed letters, visible from hundreds of yards away, gleaming above the 3,095 names engraved in white.

"Lest We Forget in gold leaf on the Ohio Vietnam Memorial Wall-OVMP archives"

When completed, the wall became the longest freestanding monument in the nation, held in place by its own weight. Joe, still president and treasurer of the park committee in May 2009, walked the length of the black granite, tracing the names from A to P. His fingers lingered over his brother Michael's name. As the dedication approached, Joe shared with local papers how emotional it was to see all the names of Ohio men and the one woman killed in action in Southeast Asia. "It's up," he said. "We still have a lot of work to do to get it paid for, but it is so satisfying that this is complete."

In time for the wall's dedication, a new welcome sign was installed at the park's entrance. A seven-foot polished black granite monument, shaped like the state of Ohio, displayed the park's name and emblem. The reverse side listed the companies, organizations, and individuals who had made the park possible, acknowledging their contributions to this important memorial.

An unusual incident unfolded in the weeks leading up to the dedication of the wall. Ken had purchased around thirty azaleas—red and white—on sale, and he and several volunteers began planting them along the walkway in front of the wall, hoping to add a touch of color to the area that hadn't yet been landscaped. Most welcomed the idea, except for Chelle, who arrived at the park and immediately started uprooting the azaleas.

A Vietnam veteran, who had spent the day planting many of them, confronted her and explained, "The white flowers symbolize purity of heart, and the red ones represent the blood of our soldiers."

Ken was there and heard Chelle snap at the volunteer, "Who are you?"

"I'm a Vietnam veteran and a volunteer," he replied.

"Well, I don't give a damn who you are! I'm a board member, and these don't belong here!" she shouted back.

She then instructed the board president, Joe, to help her remove the plants. He used his riding mower with a wagon attachment to gather the azaleas while she finished pulling them out of the ground.

"It was astounding," Ken later reflected. "I suggested we consult the board, and if they didn't like the plants, we could remove them. But she didn't listen. That volunteer left and never returned."

The dedication of the Ohio Vietnam wall took place on May 17, 2009, with a crowd of seven thousand people in attendance, according to press reports. Locals and groups from out of state gathered, many expressing that this wall and park were long overdue and finally gave Vietnam veterans the respect they deserved. Emotions were palpable even before the program began. Some visitors wiped away tears as they read the names on the wall, others bowed their heads, and all paid tribute.

"The Ohio Vietnam Memorial Wall dedication-OVMP archives"

Chapter Three

One woman from Akron admitted that she knew she would be crying all day. Veterans from WWII, Korea, and later conflicts were also present, including ninety-seven-year-old Robert Fry of Canal Fulton, who had served in WWII.

Ken recalled feeling exhilarated and deeply moved. He had hoped for a good turnout but never expected thousands. For him, the presence of one person meant everything: his father, who was there, was proud of him. That made all the hard work worthwhile.

"The Ohio Veterans Memorial Park granite welcome sign in the shape of the state-OVMP archives"

As "The Star-Spangled Banner" was sung and the flag raised around 2:20 p.m., people crossed their hearts or saluted if they were veterans. U.S. Air Force Major General Edward Mechenbier, a pilot and POW for nearly six years in North Vietnam, addressed the crowd. Then, facing the wall, he said, "I salute you. To each and every one of you, you are not forgotten."

Many color guard groups, military organizations, Scout troops, and VFWs, local and from nearby states, gathered in the cemetery across the street and formed a parade, which then marched proudly into the park for the beginning of the ceremonies.

"Smoke from the Marlboro Volunteers coming from the woods during the dedication ceremony of the Ohio Veterans Memorial Park Vietnam Wall-OVMP archives"

The Marlboro Volunteers, dressed in Vietnam-era soldier uniforms, staged a silent patrol from the nearby woods, setting off canisters of

CHAPTER THREE

colored smoke. Although expected by the park committee, it surprised visitors as the volunteers stealthily approached the wall and cut down the camouflage-designed canvas covering to unveil it, followed by a 21-gun salute.

"I can't explain it," said one tearful Vietnam veteran. "It's very emotional. It's the recognition we never got."[5]

Sergeant Johnnie Downs, who retired after serving thirty-two years across three wars in the U.S. Army, was also present. "In today's world, there are heroes. And those heroes are American soldiers," he proclaimed.

Thousands of motorcycles participated in the first annual Run to the Wall, led by Ralph Bago of the Ohio Patriot Guard Riders, John Hohne of Rolling Thunder, and Luke Patrino of the Combat Vets. The thunderous noise from a nearby town marked their arrival. Patrino, a Vietnam War veteran, stated that the day was long overdue. "I couldn't be proud of my service before. Now I feel I can be." He reminded the crowd that the project was only half finished and challenged military organizations to raise the remaining funds needed to complete it. "I say they [the park committee] have done enough. Now, it's our turn."[6]

"Visitors to the park on motorcycles-OVMP archives"

The ceremony also featured the unveiling of the *Gold Star Mother* statue. The 1,600-pound, 8.5-foot-tall Barre Gray granite monument showed a mother clutching the folded flag that had once covered her child's casket. The statue stood facing the wall, her head slightly bowed. Two Gold Star mothers—Vera Spring whose son Army Sergeant Bruce Wayne Spring was killed in Vietnam in 1970 and Julia Barkey whose son Ohio National Guard Sergeant Michael C. Barkey died in Iraq in 2004—pulled off the red, white, and blue covering.

"Gold Star Mother statue-photo credit Steve Wallis"

The Vietnam wall features the names of 3,094 men and one woman, Sharon Ann Lane. The memorial bench next to the *Gold Star*

Chapter Three

Mother statue is dedicated to her. Sharon's mother attended the Gold Star Mother ceremony.

Sharon, a first lieutenant, was an Army nurse assigned to the ICU at the 312th Evacuation Hospital in Chu Lai, Vietnam, in 1969. Born in Zanesville and raised in Canton, Ohio, she graduated from Aultman Hospital School of Nursing in 1965. Approximately eleven thousand women served in the military in Vietnam, 90 percent of them being nurses. Sharon was known for her dedication, caring for the injured during and outside of work hours, and was adored by coworkers and patients alike.

In her last letter home, she wrote about the heat, the men she cared for on Ward 4, and the movie she missed the night before. She assured her parents that mortars had not been heard for a couple of weeks at the hospital. But on June 8, 1969, a salvo of 122 mm rockets fired by the VC struck. One hit directly between Wards 4A and 4B, killing two people and injuring twenty-seven. Sharon died instantly from fragmentation wounds to the chest. She was one of eight American military nurses who died in Vietnam and the only one killed by direct hostile fire. She was buried at Sunset Hills Burial Park in Canton, Ohio, where her parents received the folded flag and numerous posthumous medals. Sharon died at the age of twenty-seven and remains an iconic representative of the sacrifice and service of the thousands of women who have served and continue to serve in the U.S. military.[7]

Near the *Gold Star Mother* statue on the wall's dedication day, Chuck Nicholas recalled a poignant incident: "I was standing by the wall talking when someone I didn't recognize at first came up and said, 'How're you doing, Charlie?' No one had called me that since high school, and I didn't take kindly to it because we called the VC in Vietnam 'Charlie.' So I said, 'Don't call me that!' It turned out to be an old high school friend, Dennis Heltsley. We grew up near each other in Akron and played sports together. I asked how he was and how his brother Paul was doing. Paul was quiet, studious, and wanted to be a doctor. He graduated with me." Chuck paused, his voice catching.

"Paul R. Heltsley-courtesy of the Heltsley family"

"Well," he continued, "Dennis told me that Paul had been killed in Vietnam. I was shocked. I went over to Panel Nine of the wall, and there was his name, Paul R. Heltsley. I fell to my knees. I watched that panel go up and didn't know his name was on it. I cried for a while."

Dennis, remembering his older brother, recounted the story: "He looked like Elvis, with dark hair styled just like that. He had hundreds of 45 records he loved to play. Paul wanted to be a doctor and was a pretty good student, but there were no jobs in the early '60s, so he enlisted." Their father worked at Goodyear Aerospace, and their mother was a

Chapter Three

stay-at-home mom, typical of that era. Paul and Dennis were the only children.

U.S. Army Private First Class Paul Robinson Heltsley III was a graduate of Akron's Garfield High School. Paul married right out of high school and had a baby daughter when he left to serve as a medical non-commissioned officer (medic) in Special Detachment 5891. Dennis described his brother's work from the letters Paul sent home. "He went on missions with doctors to treat civilians. So many of the kids had diseases like worms. He didn't like being there in Vietnam."

Dennis was only fifteen when he learned of Paul's death, and years later, it was still difficult to talk about. "Mom was home running a vacuum cleaner when the Western Union brought a telegram. I heard her scream and cry and ran to see what was wrong. It was awful . . . to be told that way. Paul had been killed. My dad was called home from work, and soon the house was filled with people, the pastor, and friends." His parents were devastated, confused, and angry. "There were only 16,000 American soldiers in Vietnam at the time," Dennis said. Paul was the first soldier from Akron to be killed in the Vietnam War. "They made such a big deal out of it—congressmen, the mayor, and dignitaries. He got the Bronze Star for heroism in ground combat, and other medals you get when you're gone. They didn't mean much to me. Paul was dead. Later, a soldier who was there with him contacted us and told us the story. He stayed in touch for many years."

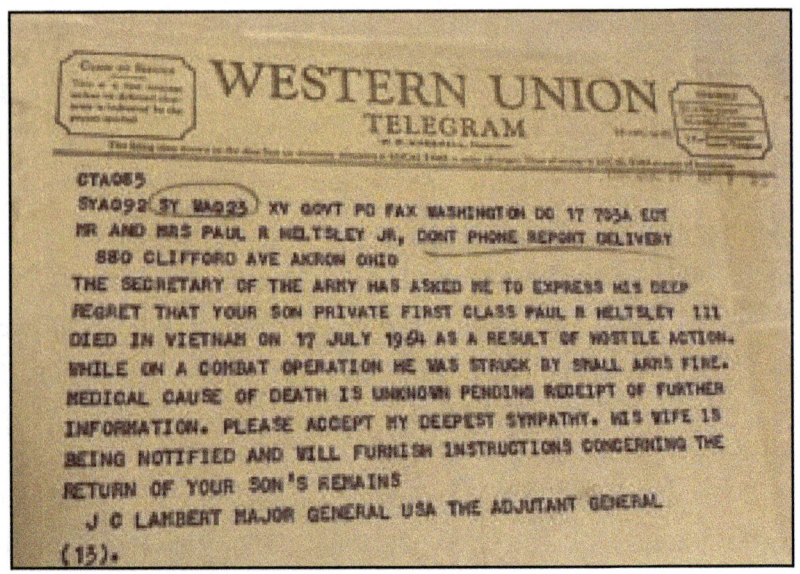

"The Western Union telegraph that had been handed to Paul's mother-courtesy of Heltsley family"

On July 17, 1964, just before dawn, Paul was killed during a combat operation. According to reports, his convoy encountered a roadblock where they were ambushed by the VC. As they tried to escape, Paul dismounted from his jeep, which was under attack, and was shot in the chest. "Shot through the heart," Dennis said. Paul had been in Vietnam for four months. He was twenty years old.

The wall dedicated that day was imposing yet intricately detailed, permanently etched with the names of young soldiers who fought for liberty and freedom. The granite symbolized strength and permanence, representing the enduring ideals of the nation.

CHAPTER THREE

"Don Maurer honoring the fallen-OVMP archives"

In the weeks that followed, the committee members were pleased with the success of drawing thousands to the park and hoped donations would continue to come in, because the wall was not yet paid for. The committee still owed over $100,000, and despite their eagerness to move forward with the next phase, they were unable to proceed.

Per the original agreement between the park committee and the Clinton Cemetery Board, the first phase of construction (the wall) had to be fully paid before starting a new phase. The new phase included the planned prisoner of war / missing in action (POW/MIA) pond. As a result, all donations were directed to paying off the wall first.

Chelle, who had been vice president for two years, continued to push for the POW/MIA pond's dedication by Veterans Day 2009. She was still actively fundraising and seeking grants, making it clear in recent emails to committee members that she was pursuing funding specifically for the pond. She even consulted a pond-building company to get a bid, which she said was much lower than Ken's estimate that he was reluctant to give her. Although Ken was not a pond builder, he was under contract to create the fifty feet of reflecting-granite wall behind the pond whenever it would be done, and he knew it would need to be a substantial feature not cheap to build.

During the May 26 meeting of that year, Chelle was told that she had not been authorized to seek bids for the pond. The committee was still overwhelmed by the outstanding debt on the wall. According to interviews and existing emails, it was made clear to Chelle at this meeting that no new funds would be allocated for the next phase of construction until the wall debt was settled.

Chelle, however, insisted that the recently promised grant money was designated specifically for the pond, not the wall, and warned that they risked losing the funds if the pond wasn't completed promptly. Later, the committee contacted the foundation that had pledged the $20,000 grant. The grantors confirmed that the money could be reserved and used later but only for the pond, and there was no immediate deadline as Chelle had suggested.

Committee members recall how frustrating the situation was. Ken had arranged for the granite supplier to extend credit for a year, but that period was nearing its end, and the pressure was mounting. Despite his involvement, Ken was not permitted to vote on financial matters related to the granite. Clearly, payments would have to be made to him over a long period of time.

Chapter Three

During the June 16 meeting, Chelle shocked Ken by suggesting, in front of everyone, that he should "write off" the remaining balance on the wall because his company had benefited from the publicity. The debt was over $100,000, and Ken vehemently disagreed. According to the park committee members present at the meeting, Chelle also argued that since the wall was already completed, it would be difficult to raise money to pay off the debt and that they should instead focus on the POW/MIA pond.

Chuck Nicholas, who was present, recalled leaning over to a committee member and exclaiming, "Did you hear that?!" Debbie Rorrer was also there and heard these statements and remembered being "flabbergasted." She stood up, slammed her notebook on the table, and shouted, "Are you kidding me?!" Debbie admitted that such a bold reaction was out of character for her, but she doubted anyone even heard her over the chaos.

Chelle Rossi resigned via email to Joe, the committee president, shortly after that. Her resignation letter was measured but cordial, stating she planned to return to see the park's progress and would come back to hand over keys and files. She mentioned attending one more meeting on June 23, which would mark her official resignation date and where she intended to transfer these items and discuss any necessary follow-up.

According to committee members and meeting minutes, Rossi did attend her final meeting, but failed to return the files belonging to the park—critical documents for ongoing projects and a future investigation. Despite repeated efforts to retrieve them, the files were never handed over. At the committee's request, Dick Elvin went to Rossi's home to collect the files after notifying her. He was known for having a friendly rapport with her. Elvin returned to the committee reporting that she refused to return the park's materials. Speaking to him at the door, she warned him: "Don't go back to the group because all hell is going to break loose." Within months, Rossi's actions would shock the park committee.

CHAPTER FOUR

Honesty is the best policy.

—Benjamin Franklin

2010

"I was completely blindsided!" Ken recalled, describing the day FBI agents from Akron, acting on behalf of the IRS, visited his office at Summit Memorials on an otherwise routine autumn day. The allegation? He was being accused of forging a signature on a contract with the 501(c)(3) organization, the Ohio Vietnam Veterans Memorial Park—the very park he had dedicated the past five years to helping build. This was just the beginning of a year-long ordeal filled with personal and organizational attacks.

"I frantically searched for the contract in question, trying to figure out where this was coming from and why," Ken said, shaking his head. He eventually met with the FBI, provided the necessary information, and was cleared. "But I had no idea what I was in for over the next few months." The next blow came by mail in early November 2009. "While I was proving that I didn't forge anyone's signature—and I did prove that," he said, "the committee and I, in particular, had been reported to the Ohio Attorney General's Office."

From October 2009 to October 2010, the park committee faced a series of negative events that left them reeling. Each new accusation felt like another blow.

The specific complaints, filed online on November 4, 2009, by Chelle Rossi, alleged issues with the 501(c)(3) status of the Ohio Vietnam Veterans Memorial Park:

- No annual audit report ever executed.
- Claims of a conflict of interest with Mr. Noon.
- Summit Memorials awarded construction without competitive bids.
- Accusations of soliciting donations and inflating costs.
- Allegations that six board members either worked directly or indirectly for Ken, received loans, were best friends, or were connected to his godchild.
- Claims of decisions made without formal meetings or proper records.
- Assertions that 9 out of 10 subcontractors were Ken's business associates, ignoring the park's best interests.

Another complaint was filed by Chelle Rossi and Luke Patrino, the motorcycle group leader who had previously praised the OVVMP at the wall dedication: "Mr. Noon, owner of Summit Memorials, is operating the Ohio Vietnam Veterans Memorial Park for the benefit of his business." They listed board members they claimed who were indebted to Ken and suggested that the closed meeting in July 2009 regarding nominations was intended to exclude Rossi as VP. However, she had already resigned from the park in June, a month before that closed meeting.

Chapter Four

During her last meeting on June 23, Rossi brought visitors from the Combat Vets motorcycle group, including Patrino. He spoke at length, questioning why the POW/MIA pond would not be completed by Veterans Day 2009. His group had planned to help fund it, but if construction wasn't going to proceed, their funds would not be forthcoming. This contentious issue seemed to have been the same one that had prompted Rossi's departure from the board the previous week.

Chuck Nicholas recalled, "I think Rossi had Patrino brainwashed." The discussion dominated the meeting, and the planned board member nominations had to be postponed, necessitating a closed meeting in July. Although meetings were generally open to the public, occasional closed sessions were deemed necessary.

In her complaint to the attorney general, Rossi wrote: "After the closed meeting . . . Ken Noon now has complete control of the Ohio Vietnam Veterans Memorial Park and all the park's money. Anyone who stands against him is run out by any means needed, as was Chelle Rossi."

Yet, the final lines of her resignation letter dated 6/16/09 to Joe Paonessa read: "MY VERY BEST TO ALL THE COMMITTEE FOR CONTINUED SUCCESS WITH THE REMAINDER TO BE BUILT AT THE PARK. THANKS FOR ALLOWING ME TO BE A PART OF IT IN THE PAST. -CHELL" (The capitalization is hers.)

According to those who were interviewed at the time and in later discussions, during her two years on the board (June 2007– June 2009), Rossi never expressed concerns to Ken or anyone else about conflicts of interest, financial misconduct, or bylaw violations. Meeting minutes do not reflect any such complaints, and despite helping the president-treasurer Joe Paonessa with taxes, she never suggested or initiated an audit. Ken maintained that he met every board member through his volunteer work at the park, not prior to joining. He also denied having a godchild. Nonetheless, the Attorney General's office was obligated to investigate these claims.

Before the attorney general's scheduled meeting in Clinton on November 24 to address the park committee's defense against these accusations, the situation took another turn, this time with negative media attention around what became known as the "fight over the Akron bench."

Bob Dyer, a general-interest columnist for the *Akron Beacon Journal*, was at the center of this media storm. In his farewell column upon retirement in 2020, he described his role at the paper: "Since 2006, I've had the best job in the newsroom—general-interest columnist. That means, essentially, that I get paid to mouth off about anything and everything . . . about 80 percent of my column ideas have come from readers. 'Hey, have you seen this?' 'Did you know this?' 'Have you heard of that?' 'What do you think of that?' "[1]

In the next few months, Bob Dyer gave the veterans park plenty of attention. In an October 2009 column, he focused on a memorial bench apparently funded by donations from Akron residents, calling it "Akron's tastelessness to last forever."[2] A "reader" had tipped him off about the bench, which had been in the park since before the May wall dedication. Interestingly, this reader only brought it to Dyer's attention in October.

After praising the inscriptions on the other thirty or so benches as "glorious," Dyer revealed Akron's bench inscription: "The city of Akron honors its Vietnam veterans - Donald L Plusquellic, Mayor." Dyer criticized the inscription as uninspired, noting that no other bench in the park featured a mayor's name. While there were benches with politicians' names, Dyer hadn't visited the park to see them himself. Ken called Dyer, suggesting that Akron was the only city represented in the park and that Akron deserved that recognition. And that other cities should step up. Dyer, however, chose to focus on the issue of the mayor's name on the bench.

Mayor Don Plusquellic, first elected in 1987, had his share of critics, particularly among *Akron Beacon Journal* readers. Earlier in 2009, he survived a recall election and cleared his name after accusations of a DUI and a hit-and-run, which he claimed were politically motivated.

The inscription on Akron's bench was a simple misunderstanding. Those responsible for the wording thought it was akin to a plaque or marker, which often included a mayor's name. In a subsequent column on November 3, titled "New words in the works for the bench,"[3] Dyer reported that the park planned to change the inscription. Though a new bench was eventually installed, the controversy didn't end there.

Dyer's column "Infighting mars park for visitors"[4] on December 15 was based on information from a "reader" who claimed the bench had been relocated to a less visible location. However, a park spokesperson later clarified that the bench had not been moved to a less prominent spot. It was still in front of the wall next to the *Gold Star Mother* statue. It seemed that someone was stirring up controversy.

Rossi's name appeared in this particular column (as Dyer referenced her complaints to the attorney general), stating the park had "numerous issues." Even Dan Delarosa, who had not been involved for years, was quoted, saying the situation "breaks my heart." According to Dyer, Delarosa claimed his falling out with the park occurred in 2006, citing concerns over board members spending money without proper approval. He accused Noon of "lining his pockets." Dyer suggested that the split seemed irreparable.

Ken recalled how unsettling it was to read Dan's comments, if reported accurately. "It triggered feelings of dread. I felt alone. I was continually being attacked." Committee members were frustrated and not all of them were supportive of Ken, and those who hadn't resigned were angry about the entire situation.

Meanwhile, it was revealed that Rossi and Patrino had scheduled their own organizational meeting on November 18 for the "2nd Annual Run to the Vietnam Veterans Memorial Wall," planned for July 2010. The park committee knew nothing about this event, as they had intended to organize it themselves. Patrino claimed, in a letter, that he was the "owner and organizer" of the first annual "Run to the Ohio Vietnam Veterans Wall," which took place during the wall dedication. He believed this gave him the right to lead the second run.

Motorcycle poker runs were a popular way for the park to raise funds, with entry fees and raffles generating donations. The veteran motorcycle groups were generous, and the park relied on their support. The park committee believed that the first run was a collaborative effort organized by many, with Patrino leading it—but not owning it. Patrino's plan was to bring three thousand motorcycles to the wall in July 2010 to honor veterans. Until this point, they were unaware that a new organization was being formed to manage the ride, now renamed "Run to the Ohio Wall."

The park committee found themselves under siege, trying to connect the dots behind the attacks against them. After their meeting with the attorney general (AG), they had to await a critical decision regarding their 501(c)(3) status, knowing a thorough audit of their finances was imminent. With Christmas 2009 approaching, they turned their focus to the holiday season and planned a major fundraiser for January. The work continued, despite the mounting challenges.

In early December 2009, scathing articles criticizing the park began appearing in local newspapers, including in Akron where Ken's business was based. "I felt my business and my personal reputation were targeted." The park committee quickly mobilized, with local papers offering them space for rebuttals, and a war of words ensued.[5]

Bob Dyer wrote another article, "Feuding Scars Veterans Memorial."[6] Meanwhile Ann Kagarise of *The Suburbanite* contributed with an article, "A War Over the Wall Brews in Clinton."[7] "Ohio Vietnam Veterans Memorial Being Hijacked"[8] and other letters to the editor from Rossi and responses from the park committee fueled the ongoing debate.[9]

The committee drafted a general response to address these accusations, using much of the same material prepared for the AG meeting. It was a difficult and draining period, though they felt they had successfully defended their position.

In December, a new voice joined the fray—Veterans-For-Change, a national online group from California that advocates for veterans' issues. An article titled "Ohio Vietnam Veterans Memorial Park"[10] by Rossi was published on their platform, where she had found a sympathetic ear. The piece reiterated her complaints: the park's "refusal" to construct the POW/MIA memorial, accusations of conflicts of interest, and claims of no-bid contracts with Ken's company. Toward the end, she introduced a new accusation. Despite not attending the AG meeting on November 24, 2009, in Clinton, she claimed, "Noon presented a written contract allegedly signed by Dan Delarosa as president of OVVMP, 2006," and that the AG "did not question the validity of the signature, even after Dan had contacted them."

How had she known that Dan had contacted the AG's office?

The contract in question was one that Dan had asked Ken to draft in February 2006 for the 501(c)(3) application, explicitly listing Summit Memorials as the chosen company to build the monument.

This contract expired in June 2006 with no money exchanged, as no property had been secured by that time. A renewed contract was signed by the park's president Joe Paonessa in 2008 for the Clinton property where the park was eventually built.

The attorney general's office concluded that Ken had no reason to forge Dan's signature, especially since Dan had initially requested the contract. Ken was even advised that he could pursue legal action against those who made the accusations against him, but he chose not to. "I was angry and disappointed, but I was exhausted. It was reflecting badly on the park, and I just wanted it to be over." Unfortunately, the turmoil was far from over.

In early January 2010, Akron's Mayor Don Plusquellic's deputy Dave Lieberth requested a meeting with Frank Sasz, the park's president at the time. He was going to turn over the donation check for the bench. Lieberth asked Sasz to "bring Mr. Noon along." Ken was puzzled over his purpose in joining this meeting.

"We had coffee at McDonald's," Ken recalled. "Lieberth slid a letter across the table, dated December 21, 2009, addressed to Mayor Plusquellic."

As Ken read the letter, he was confounded. It was purportedly a business letter from Summit Memorials, personally signed by him, on company stationery—but it was a photocopy, not on original stationery. Two things immediately stood out: Ken had been in Canada on a fishing trip when the letter was supposedly sent, and the content was entirely unfamiliar. The letter read like a desperate sales pitch:

Chapter Four

Mayor Donald Plusquellic,

As a valued customer, we have some exciting news. The cost of the material used in the Memorial Benches has risen sharply due to our use of a new supplier. With the $500.00 increase, the cost has risen to $4,000.00. To make up for the increase, we will offer a $250.00 trade-in for your used bench. As a holiday extra, we are offering a $100.00 rebate on new benches. The cost of your new bench will be $3,650.00 instead of $4,000.00. Your original spot at the entrance of the Memorial Wall next to the 'Gold Star Mother' statue was given by the OVMP Committee to the Village of Clinton. You will have your choice of the three remaining spaces behind the Memorial Wall.

This offer expires 5:00 P.M. 8 January, 2010. This offer is only available to our most valued customers. Thanks for doing business with Summit Memorials. Merry Christmas and Happy New Year. —Ken Noon, President.

P.S. You can meet with Charles Olminsky (My Attorney) and Myself at the Cliffside Tavern corner of S. Main St. and Waterloo Rd. most afternoons after 5:00 P.M. We can discuss our easy payment plan over a drink, first one on Me."

Ken was stunned. The letter not only sounded unprofessional but also insinuated shady dealings. The situation left him more confused and worried about the escalating attacks. Summit Memorials never directly sold those park benches. The OVVMP handled sales and contracted

Summit Memorials to design and install them. Ken's company never solicited business in the manner suggested by the fake letter.

Upon obtaining the letter, Ken immediately consulted his longtime secretary Barbara. She didn't recognize it, but they noticed the stationery used was outdated and missing the company's website under the logo. Barbara pointed out that it must have been copied from older stationery, confirming Ken's suspicion that he was being set up. Determined to get to the bottom of it, Ken went directly to Mayor Plusquellic's office hoping to obtain the original letter. "I knew I was being targeted," he said.

Ken was aware that the letter's P.S. suggesting a meeting at a bar was a jab at him, implying he could be found there daily, and also a dig at the mayor, playing off recent false DUI allegations against Plusquellic. Ken waited four hours before meeting with the mayor, who handed him the original letter. It was also a photocopy, not on genuine stationery. Mayor Plusquellic had placed it in a file for "trash" letters. Ken remarked, "If the mayor needed granite, I wouldn't have been at the top of the list of preferred vendors!"

Ken observed that the letter appeared to have been produced on a copy machine, with tiny fibers visible around a patch of text in the center, indicating someone had taped a smaller piece of paper onto Summit Memorials' letterhead before copying it. "I could prove it in court, but I didn't pursue it. I kept it as evidence, just in case," Ken noted.

Mayor Plusquellic also revealed that other politicians, many of whom had attended park events, had received similar letters defaming Summit Memorials and Ken. His concerns about his business and reputation were well founded.

In early 2010, after a thorough audit, the park's attorney notified the committee that no infractions were found and all accusations were dismissed by the attorney general's office. However, as a matter of policy, the AG did not publicly comment on closed or ongoing cases. This left room for misinformation to spread, allowing Rossi to continue her campaign on the national platform Veterans-For-Change. She disseminated her accusations on other veteran sites, including the *Canada Free Press*, claiming, "The Ohio AG's office did not excuse OVVMP; quite the contrary, they are investigating new suspect activity... There is also a federal investigation underway despite what the OVVMP committee thinks or says."[11]

In reality, the AG's office had concluded its investigation and was growing weary of Rossi's persistent complaints. Articles in Veterans-For-Change amplified her claims, and several park committee members tried to contact the website's columnist Jim Davis to clarify the situation. Emails reveal their attempts to correct the record, but Davis sided with Rossi. On December 22, 2009, he sent an email to the board via Summit Memorials, demanding:

> Immediate action be taken to dismantle the entire current board of the organization and replace it with a board of veterans who care for and about and will honor this memorial with the dignity and respect it so richly deserves...
>
> Below, I have as a courtesy pasted the story which I released on Sunday, December 21, 2009, to an estimated 15,000 veterans nationwide, which will be followed by a press release to an estimated 6,400 members of the media to further highlight the mismanagement of the Veterans Memorial Project and what a disgrace this is.

I will also be making several calls this week to key members in both the Senate and the House, as well as the Department of Justice, and please be assured I nor the members of our organization will be dropping or walking away from this very important issue.

What I'd like to receive within the next 7 days is a formal letter informing me that all board members of the Vietnam Veterans Memorial Park Board will or have resigned, a full accounting of all donated and expended funds, and all missing funds replaced by said board members.[12]

The story he referenced was Rossi's piece, reiterating her complaints and including claims about the POW/MIA pond being delayed and accusations of $20,000 in grant money gone "missing." In truth, the funds were moved to a new account after Rossi's resignation because she still had access to the original account. Her claims that the funds were missing stemmed from her inability to see the new account's details.

The park committee, still reeling from the negative press, began to understand the situation better and chose not to be threatened by Rossi or Davis. Disappointed, they noted how quickly people believed the worst, especially from a national platform like Veterans-For-Change lending credibility to Rossi's accusations.

On January 7, 2010, Rossi escalated matters further by filing a complaint with the Better Business Bureau, claiming, "NOON DID NOT CARVE THE STATUE," referring to the Gold Star Mother monument. This was the same statue Ken had been working on when he was publicly photographed just a year earlier when Rossi had expressed confidence that people would "fall in love" with the park. In her BBB complaint, she accused Summit Memorials of "deceptive advertising."

The BBB, however, chose not to process the complaint formally, informing Ken by letter: "Because of the nature of the complaint, we are not processing it as a formal complaint." Ken was left bewildered, wondering, "What is Rossi's problem?"

Amidst all this turmoil, the committee was also debating a potential name change for the park, from "Ohio Vietnam Veterans Memorial Park" to "Ohio Veterans Memorial Park: Home of the Ohio Vietnam Veterans Memorial Wall." The idea had been around for a couple of years, and the intention was to expand the park's scope to honor veterans from other wars, using the remaining space on the back of the wall for additional names. However, this idea stirred mixed feelings. Some Vietnam veterans felt slighted.

"Some no longer felt they could volunteer for the park," said Don Maurer, a Vietnam veteran who remained with the project.

Delmer Milhoan left the park over the decision to change its name. "There are other veterans memorials all over the state. This was ours. This was for my buddies who died. I just couldn't understand why they had to drop 'Vietnam' from the name. I felt it was ordained by God to keep it." He departed before the wall was completed and dedicated.

While many Vietnam veterans often spoke of honoring Korean War veterans and supported existing and upcoming monuments for the Medal of Honor, Purple Heart, POW/MIA, and the Gold Star Father, there were also new conflicts and recent losses. The official name change to the Ohio Veterans Memorial Park (OVMP) was voted on and passed in April 2010. According to Ken, Rossi had advocated for this change when she was still on the park committee, believing it would help fundraising efforts. It did indeed boost donations significantly. Yet, once the change was official, a seed was planted that the park committee was trying to collect funds under both names, attempting to stir further controversy.

Meanwhile, plans for the second Run to the Wall were progressing, and park committee members attended the planning meetings when possible. They were told they were welcome. However, during a January meeting, Luke Patrino informed a park committee member that none of the funds raised by the Run would go to the park, even though many motorcycles would likely attend ceremonies there. When asked why, Patrino cited ongoing investigations by the AG and the IRS against the park. What wasn't mentioned at the meeting was that it was Patrino and his secretary, Rossi, who had filed the complaints.

The park committee recognized that a large event like the Run could be costly for them. Over the following months, tensions escalated as logistical issues arose. The Clinton Cemetery Board, which controlled the surrounding land, was concerned about parking and insisted that additional insurance should be covered by the Ohio Run to the Wall organization. Clinton's safety commission required the park's permission for events with more than 250 visitors and requested adherence to certain rules and safety protocols. Additionally, the village of Clinton wanted police protection for the anticipated three thousand motorcycles and the costs to be borne by the Run organization. Since Clinton did not have its own police force, the New Franklin law director, who oversaw shared services, asked for a meeting with the Run organizers to discuss logistics.

The situation quickly deteriorated. The Run organization, which agreed to a couple of the requests, felt their efforts were being unnecessarily obstructed and refused to meet with the New Franklin law director, arguing that the event was in Clinton, not New Franklin. They accused the veterans park of being "petty" because donations from the Run would not be shared with them. The disagreement spilled into the newspapers, prompting communities to take sides. The OVMP Committee accused the Run organizers of pushing their agenda without regard for the concerns of other stakeholders.

In April, the park committee was further blindsided when they were notified that an Ohio civil rights affidavit had been filed by Luke Patrino against the OVMP, alleging denial of "public accommodation due to his military status and in retaliation for complaining about the respondent's policies." The case was quickly dismissed, but not before the park committee had to engage legal representation. Little did they know, another lawsuit was brewing.

A week before the second Run to the Wall was scheduled, it remained uncertain whether it would take place. The arguments had only intensified. Suddenly, the park committee was hit with another lawsuit naming the OVMP Committee, the New Franklin law director, two trustees of the Clinton Cemetery Association, the mayor of Clinton, and, unsurprisingly, Ken Noon.

"There was no time to recover from one hit before the next one," Ken recalled. "It made me feel crazy. Then I would be crazy trying to prove I wasn't crazy."

The plaintiffs in the lawsuit were no surprise either: Patrino and Rossi, both individually and as officers of the Run to the Ohio Vietnam Veterans Memorial Wall, Inc., along with other unnamed members participating in the event. They believed the defendants were trying to stop the Run. A few days before the Run, scheduled for the weekend of July 24–25, they gathered in the courtroom. Conspicuously absent was Rossi, who had been colleagues and friends with many of those present from Clinton and the surrounding communities. Her behavior puzzled them.

"I don't understand why she is doing this," said Mayor Phyllis Mayberry of Clinton.

After considering the arguments, the judge concluded that he did not wish to disrupt an event where veterans intended to honor the memorial wall. He reasoned that, as they had been present for the wall's dedication the previous year, there was no need to raise an issue now. Thus, the 2nd Annual Run to the Wall was permitted to proceed.

Despite the plaintiffs' legal victory, the turnout was modest. Only a few hundred motorcycles showed up; one park member counted just 250. On the following Tuesday, July 27, the plaintiffs' attorney dismissed the lawsuit. Rossi continued her negative press campaign against the park committee. While meeting minutes reveal the committee discussed ways to counter her actions, ultimately they chose not to pursue any.

After months of turmoil, the park committee received a long-awaited letter in October that marked the end of Rossi's efforts. The Ohio Attorney General's Office addressed her most recent complaint, dated October 4, 2010, and reiterated, "As stated in our earlier letters of 07/07/10 and 09/10/10, the issues that you have presented here have been thoroughly investigated and warrant no further action by our office."

That same month, Ken sent Bob Dyer that letter from the AG's office and Dyer then published a piece titled "Light shines on fight in Clinton,"[13] which finally offered some clarity on the issue. "She told me," Dyer wrote about Rossi, "the Ohio Attorney General was hot on their heels . . . The AG sent a letter to Rossi telling her to go away." It was the last column he would write on the matter, having realized the unfounded nature of Rossi's claims.

As promised to Ken, Dyer concluded his October column by an announcement: "At least one side is moving ahead. At 3 p.m. on

November 13, the park will dedicate a major expansion, the POW/MIA Reflection Pond, and light an eternal flame. This phase is being done in stages. The pond and landscaping are in place and paid for, but more funding is needed for the fifty-foot wall expected in 2011."

And move ahead they did.

Ironically, the very expansion Rossi had pushed for the previous year was now being completed. With the cemetery board's permission to proceed to the next phase, as the wall was being paid for, the park volunteers began digging the pond themselves. A pond builder's plans were purchased for $200, and by that summer, work was underway. The pond, measured fifty feet long and about fifteen feet wide. It was two to three feet deep and featured a concrete foundation to house the eternal flame, which appeared to float on the water. It held approximately ten thousand gallons of water, a liner, and black dye to create a reflective surface that mirrored the sky.

The pond's design was deliberate. Fifty feet long, it would one day be mirrored by a matching fifty-foot black granite wall behind it. Surrounded by colorful landscaping, the pond took on a natural, appealing shape. A four-tiered, twenty-five-foot cascading waterfall over large rocks, powered by hidden pumps, flowed gracefully into it. A sloped brick walkway with a sitting area and memorial benches led down to the water's edge.

The highlight was the eternal flame, set within an inverted powder-coated steel pot helmet donated by the Ohio Patriot Guard Riders motorcycle group. The tribute to all POW/MIA soldiers featured a black granite replica of the POW/MIA flag, inscribed with the words "Until they all come home."

"The eternal flame in the POW pond-OVMP archives"

Originally fueled by propane, the flame was later switched to a gas line. Though the black granite wall wouldn't be added for nearly three more years, the dedication of the POW/MIA Reflection Pond and Eternal Flame on November 13, 2010, was a significant achievement. This marked the first major expansion of the park beyond its role as the Home of the Ohio Vietnam Wall, setting the stage for a broader, more inclusive tribute to veterans.

CHAPTER FIVE

The torch; be yours to hold it high.
If ye break faith with us who die
We shall not sleep, though poppies grow
In Flanders fields.

—John McCrae, *"In Flanders Fields"*

2011–2012

At the northern end of the back of the Ohio Vietnam Wall, the conflicts since the Vietnam War are listed, along with the death tolls for Ohio service members. The loss of life across our country is profound, and it is vital to remember those who have sacrificed in more recent wars as well.

U.S. Totals:[1]

- **The Beirut Bombing (October 23, 1983):** 241 military personnel, including 220 Marines, dead
- **The Gulf War, Invasion of Iraq:**
    - Operation Desert Shield / Desert Storm (August 2, 1990–February 28, 1991): 147 deaths
- **War on Terrorism (2001–present):**

- Operation Iraqi Freedom (March 19, 2003–August 31, 2010): 4,431 deaths

- Operation New Dawn (September 1, 2010–December 31, 2011): 74 deaths

- Operation Enduring Freedom, *Afghanistan only* (October 7, 2001–December 31, 2014): 2,219 deaths; with other locations worldwide, an additional 131 deaths

- Operation Freedom's Sentinel (2014–2021): 109 deaths

- Operation Inherent Resolve (2014–present): 111 deaths

In more recent conflicts, advancements in medical care have allowed many catastrophic injuries to be survivable, resulting in fewer overall deaths. Yet the loss of one son or daughter in battle remains an unimaginable tragedy—a desolate journey for parents and families, no matter how much time passes. Each family must be met where they are in their grief, balancing the pain of outliving their children and finding sacred ways to honor their memory.

Chapter Five

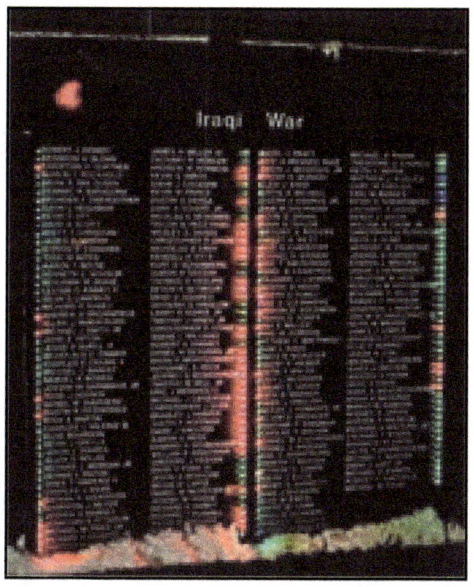

"Christmas lights attached to each name to depict branch of service by color-OVMP archives"

It would be hard to find a soldier more honored in the years since his passing in Iraq than Eric M. Barnes. Over the seventeen years since his death, his name has been memorialized with numerous awards, posthumous medals, a marble cross, a boardroom named in his honor, a carved eagle in his hometown, and streets named after him across the globe. His likeness has been captured in various artworks, including a near-life-size painting on a brick building in his home county.

"Not a single year has gone by," said his father, Tom Barnes, "without a plaque, a visit, or an invitation in Eric's honor. We receive gifts from strangers or anonymously, and it's really astounding. And heartwarming." Eric's mother, Shary Barnes, echoed these sentiments, adding that the outpouring of love has been a source of comfort over the years. "The other Gold Star Mothers have also been unbelievably gracious and supportive to me," she shared.

Born in 1986 and raised in Lorain, Ohio, Eric was a typical boy who loved baseball, NASCAR, and the outdoors. He was a big brother to Dale, just twenty-two months younger. Though they had their share of sibling rivalry growing up, Dale became Eric's best friend. Eric was known for his easygoing nature, his loyalty to his friends, and his ability to make friends wherever he went.

In school, he played in the band and once confided to his mother that the main reason he stuck with it was the chance to join the band on trips to Disney World. He also persevered through the ranks of scouting to become an Eagle Scout. Caring and honest, Eric possessed a sharp sense of humor that once saved him from a sergeant's wrath in boot camp. His father recalled that a sergeant, wanting to reprimand Eric for insubordination, found himself laughing too hard to carry through with it.

"Eric wanted to be in the Air Force since he was a young boy, so there was no stopping him from enlisting right out of high school. We certainly didn't try to stop him. He went after it. That's how he was," said Tom, who had served in the Navy.

Chapter Five

"Airforce Airman 1st Class, Eric M. Barnes-courtesy of the Barnes family"

A strikingly handsome young man, Eric posed for a portrait in his uniform before deployment. His mother had teased him, insisting he smile and show his pearly whites, and he obliged. During training at Francis E. Warren Air Force Base in Cheyenne, Wyoming, Eric excelled, demonstrating strong leadership qualities. Well liked by both staff and fellow soldiers, he stood out not only because of his six-foot, six-inch frame but also because of his infectious personality, earning him the nickname "Joker."

Eric trained as a truck driver in Missouri and embarked on his first tour to Arifjan, Kuwait, in April 2006. Serving with the 424 Medium Truck Detachment, he ran convoy operations, delivering supplies along perilous roads. After completing his tour, he returned to F.E. Warren AFB in November 2006, then came home to Ohio for a brief visit. During that time, Eric shared unexpected news with his family: He had volunteered for a second tour of duty. Among the returning soldiers, he was the only one who chose to go back, and his parents later learned that his peers had tried to dissuade him from returning to the Middle East.

Neither his peers nor his family could change Eric's mind. Even his commanding officer, whose approval Eric needed, was unsuccessful in convincing him to stay. The CO later recounted to Eric's parents that Eric had persistently visited his office, pushing for permission to redeploy, until the CO finally banned him from returning for three days. But Eric was undeterred. After the brief ban, he went right back to the CO's office, asking once again to go back on duty. Eventually, his CO relented.

"*Eric Barnes at work-courtesy of the Barnes family*"

Chapter Five

"Eric told him that people didn't believe we were doing good over there, but he knew that we were," recalled his father with a mix of pride and sadness. Eric went back to Missouri for further truck-driving training, and his second tour to Iraq began in April 2007.

On June 10, 2007, a Sunday, at 2:30 a.m., there was a knock at the Barneses' family home.

"Never a good thing at that time of the morning," Tom said. "And really not a good thing when you see two high-ranking, uniformed officers on your porch. I immediately knew Eric was dead." He had to wake Shary and Dale to tell them. "The officers had driven up from Wright-Patterson Air Force Base as soon as they got the news. They stayed maybe half an hour. They couldn't add much after they told us his truck had driven over an improvised explosive device (IED), a roadside bomb."

"I didn't get to see his body or say goodbye to my boy," Shary said tearfully.

In the days, weeks, and months that followed, the Barnes family was enveloped in an outpouring of love and support. Multitudes rallied around them, offering strength during their darkest moments. Hundreds attended Eric's funerals, both in Lorain and Wyoming, as ceremonies and tributes honored his sacrifice. The support was overwhelming, with people from all walks of life—those who had known Eric personally, and others who had only heard his story—coming forward to express their condolences and admiration. Many of Eric's military friends continue to visit the Barneses' home, often staying for a few days, something that brings immense comfort to his parents.

One person Tom hopes to meet someday is the soldier who asked Eric to switch places and let them drive on the night of the incident.

Eric had agreed, and it was the passenger side of the truck, where Eric was sitting, that took the full impact of the IED.

"This soldier was injured terribly, but the wounds he feels inside are just as bad or worse," Tom said. "He feels guilty about wanting to drive and about trading places with Eric. He spoke to me on the phone, but I want him to come here. I want to hold him and tell him that it wasn't his fault. He needs that."

That's a father speaking. A Gold Star father.

The park's walkways gradually filled with beautiful memorial benches, each a testament to the memories of those who served. These benches, along with engraved bricks and donations, played a crucial role in helping fund the wall and ensuring it could be paid off. The Akron bench was redesigned with much more thought and care, reflecting a deeper sense of reverence. This time, the city invited submissions that would honor veterans, receiving over sixty suggestions. A team of three was chosen to create the final design.

Rick McPherson, a Vietnam veteran and retired Akron police officer, proposed the quote from Major Michael O'Donnell, a U.S. Army helicopter pilot who was killed when his aircraft was shot down on March 24, 1970. The words, now engraved on the top left of the bench's back, read: "If you are able, save a place for them inside you and save one backward glance when you are leaving for the places they can no longer go."

Etched next to it is an image of a female Marine bugler (an idea by Lynee Hillegas) holding a scroll with the words of "Taps." The depiction was based on the artist Ken Noon's friend Elva Pounders who served as a Marine bugler. The front of the bench seat carries the inscription: "The City of Akron, Ohio, remembers their Vietnam War veterans," a suggestion by Tammy Gilbersleeve. Other committee members involved

CHAPTER FIVE

in the design process included George Baker and Laura Williams Dunlap. The redesigned bench has become a proud symbol of Akron's commitment to honoring its Vietnam veterans and still sits prominently near the *Gold Star Mother* statue.

One of the most thrilling projects for the park volunteers was bringing in and displaying the AH-1 Cobra helicopter. The OVMP had long been on the U.S. Army Tank-Automotive and Armaments Command, or TACOM, list to receive a UH-1 Huey helicopter, a larger aircraft than the Cobra, for display. The Huey, an iconic aircraft known for the distinctive *WA-WA-WA-WA* sound of its forty-eight-foot rotor blades, had played a critical role in the Vietnam War, saving countless lives. It was also the inspiration behind the park, connected to the story of Jesse Delarosa and the Huey he piloted as described in Chapter One. However, in 2010, the park committee was informed that due to the Ohio Attorney General's investigation—despite the charges being dismissed—they had been moved lower on the list and were unlikely to receive the Huey anytime soon. The hope of acquiring one from them remained faint but alive.

"Accompanying the Cobra helicopter into the park-OVMP archives"

In the meantime, the Cobra helicopter had become a striking feature of the park. This aircraft, first deployed in Vietnam in September 1967, had a primary mission of providing fire support to protect the Huey helicopters carrying American troops. It was a reassuring sight for American and allied soldiers, but a menacing one for the enemy, who dubbed it "Silent Death," while Americans affectionately called it "The Snake." Approximately three hundred of these helicopters were lost to combat during the Vietnam War, but the Cobra's legacy endures, now proudly on display at the park as a reminder of those who served and the machines that played a vital role in their missions.[2]

The Cobra aircraft was discovered in poor condition in a field near the Muskingum River in Zanesville, Ohio, about a hundred yards from the water. It had served in Vietnam, completing nearly one hundred tours, with its last station being the USS *Eisenhower*. The aircraft was covered in green moss, infested with hornets, and entangled in weeds, making the task of loading it onto a flatbed truck for transport to Clinton quite challenging.

A small group of the park committee visited the Cobra a couple of times. Frank Sasz, an Army veteran of 30 years, was president of the park committee then. He was a popular man at the park and received the Ohio Veteran of Year right before his retirement from the board. He was accompanied on this trip by Chuck and a couple of other members.

Chuck recalled, "Several of us were stung numerous times before it was cleaned out. Frank got stung twelve times but refused to seek emergency care."

The team made multiple trips to prepare the Cobra for its hundred-mile journey. In October 2011, under the cover of a foggy early morning, the aircraft embarked on its final mission. A long flatbed truck carefully navigated its way to Clinton, escorted by the state highway patrol and

Chapter Five

hundreds of motorcycles—half leading the way and the rest following behind. The journey was a spectacle, as the forty-four-foot-long fuselage, without its rotors attached, measured just over ten feet wide and thirteen and a half feet high. The rotor blades themselves were also forty-four feet long, and the single engine was still housed within the fuselage of the helicopter.

The route, chosen primarily for highway travel, was carefully planned, but as dawn broke, the truck's size and the sight of the convoy created quite a stir at intersections. Despite the challenges, the transport was completed safely. Many of the Zanesville veterans, at the VFW post where the Cobra sat for years, had helped load the Cobra. A few accompanied it to its new home in Clinton. Initially, some were unhappy to see the helicopter leave, but after visiting the Ohio Vietnam Wall and the park, those few changed their minds. They told committee members, "The Cobra is home."

"Lifting the Cobra into place with a crane-OVMP archives"

Mike Murphy, working for the company Selinsky Force who generously provided the crane and machinery for the job, was ready to unload the aircraft onto a concrete pad. For security reasons, the helicopter had to be disabled before it could be displayed; a V-cut was made through the engine mounts to ensure it could never be flown while displayed. It also needed to be cleaned and prepared for display, as it was initially quite rough looking. But once lowered onto the concrete, it had finally found its place.

With the fuselage repainted in iconic Army green, two helmeted mannequins were seated inside—one as the gunner in the front and the other as the pilot behind. Ken, the resident artist of the group, painted a large shark's grin around the nose, a design inspired by images he'd seen of Cobras in Vietnam. He also added painted pipes to simulate the missing armament on the outer fuselage. The plan was to eventually mount the helicopter on a permanent pedestal. When the time came, the crane returned to lift it into place, positioning it six feet off the ground, angled as if it were flying through the air. The Huey helicopter, when it was obtained, would be at that height or higher coming in behind it.

Chuck still holds onto a dream of adding lights to the display, saying, "So at night, anyone looking over the park at night will see it soaring."

It took many volunteers to help position the helicopter. A person who was there assisting was a longtime volunteer at the park, Richard Baum, who has been involved since he offered to make street signs for the park in 2008, as he worked in highway safety. A friend of his, who often visited the park, introduced him to it. Rich, who is from the area, served in the Army from 1968 to 1971 and was stationed in Europe.

A close friend of Richard's from elementary through high school, Erwin "Bruce" Sims, had been drafted into the service as a conscientious

Chapter Five

objector, a designation given to those whose personal beliefs are incompatible with military service. Bruce served as a medic in Vietnam and did not carry a gun. Tragically, a month after returning to Vietnam from leave he was killed. At his funeral, Rich was told he was shot by a sniper in Saigon in February 1968.

Rich had just seen Bruce during his leave, making the news of his death especially upsetting. Shortly after, Rich himself was headed to basic training. For many years, he tried to push the memory of Bruce's death out of his mind. He recalled volunteering at the park a number of years ago, and a young woman and her daughter stopped by. She asked about the wall and stated she was looking for her uncle's name. Her uncle happened to be Bruce Sims.

She knew very little about her uncle's death. Her father, Bruce's younger brother, knew nothing, and both he and his father would never talk about Bruce's death. This made Rich want to know more, so he researched online about Bruce's service in Vietnam.

Private First Class (E3) E. Bruce Sims was a medic assigned to the 3rd Platoon, "C" Company, 1st Battalion. He was flown in to assist the 3rd Platoon, which had come under fire encountering North Vietnamese Army soldiers hiding in a hedgerow. The platoon had nearly landed on top of the NVA battalion. During the intense conflict, Bruce was attempting to administer aid and was killed alongside the soldiers he was trying to help.

This story is still difficult for Rich to share, but working at the park has been a healing experience for him and for others who carry similar memories. One day while volunteering, Rich noticed a man who kept returning to the memorial wall sobbing. The man would walk to the wall, then back to where a woman waited near the parking lot, only to return and cry again. The woman, his wife, approached Rich and asked for advice. "What should I do? He just cries," she said.

Rich suggested that if her husband approached one of the volunteers, she should step away and give them space to talk. He explained that the man needed someone to confide in but wasn't ready to share his inner struggle with her yet. Perhaps, in time, he would be able to. These situations were not unusual at the park.

"The Ohio Vietnam Wall in the evening-photo credit Steve Wallis"

Even with daily volunteers helping with tasks at the park, it takes strategic planners and coordinators to handle the heavy lifting of planning and of the implementation of fundraising efforts. For many years after the Rossi debacle, Sharon Kerechanin played this crucial role for the OVMP. Her dedication was deeply personal, as her late husband, George, was a Vietnam U.S. Army veteran. As a widow, Sharon had balanced work and raising her children, but once she was able to, she made the park her cause.

Sharon took grant-writing classes, and she often remarked that researching potential donors consumed more time than the actual grant

Chapter Five

writing. But her efforts paid off, as she successfully secured funds from private institutions and through numerous fundraising activities over the years. The park was in dire need of having the parking lot and the circle road paved because the limestone surface caused issues, especially for motorcyclists who often kicked up dust and voiced their complaints. Sharon navigated numerous hurdles to secure a grant from a corporation, ultimately making the much-needed paving project possible.

She was a skilled event coordinator, organizing everything from Christmas tree lightings and patriotic holiday observances to large-scale events like the motorcycle rides. One of the most notable was the annual Run to the Wall, which included 5K, 10K, and half-marathon races. It attracted up to four hundred participants to walk or run, with thousands of spectators cheering them on. Volunteers contributed to its success by designing clever T-shirts and crafting unique medals, which were presented during fun ceremonies for the winners.

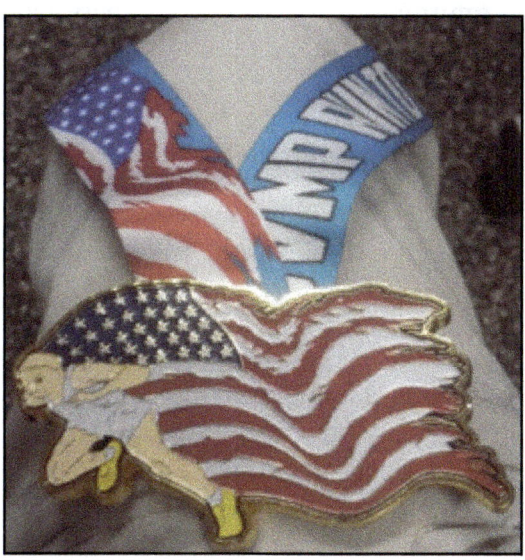

"A medal given for Run to the Wall race-OVMP archives"

Sharon's ability to connect with neighboring communities and forge alliances was key to securing the support needed for these events, including the building of the Family of Heroes Hall. A dedicated team of volunteers and supporters worked alongside her ensuring that the park continued to thrive and serve as a place of remembrance and honor.

Carol Parker Park, a dedicated leader in the Disabled American Veterans (DAV) organization for over thirty years, also found time to devote to the OVMP. With a deep family connection to military service—her father, Sergeant Homer R. Parker of the Army Air Corps was a survivor of the Pearl Harbor attack by the Japanese at the start of World War II—she has long been involved with a chapter of the Pearl Harbor Survivors Association. She credits her father with instilling in her a profound respect for the country and the flag. Her connection to the OVMP began over a decade ago when the Pearl Harbor group made a donation to the park, sparking her ongoing involvement.

Carol's commitment to veterans is also personal: Her husband Jack (U.S. Air Force) and brother John (USMC) are both Vietnam War veterans. John was a national service officer for the DAV in California and Ohio with thirty-eight years' service and continues helping even through serious health issues, including near blindness from strokes. He lives with Carol and Jack, and as she said, they are all a great team.

She volunteers at the park whenever she can and has served on the park committee for many years. She has a particular passion for advocating for female veterans, recognizing that "they have special needs, and there are so many more women veterans as the years go by." Her efforts continue to ensure that the park honors and supports all who have served.

CHAPTER FIVE

"The barn, sandblasted, painted with the addition of the crying eagle to honor victims of 9/11"

In 2010, the cemetery board purchased a distinctive old barn located at the edge of the property. The acquisition was driven by a need for shelter for the cemetery's riding mowers, as well as offering storage space for the park, which had begun accumulating larger equipment. The barn's exterior, clad in wide, weathered wooden planks, had endured decades of exposure but remained solid. Its steeply pitched roof would need to be replaced to keep the interior dry. The structure was painted white with bold red stripes wrapping around it, a blue section resembling the U.S. flag, and an enormous eagle's head with a tear in its eye a few years ago with permission of the cemetery board.

The barn, sturdy and well built, features large wooden double doors at the south end, wide enough to accommodate maintenance equipment. The lower level has a hardened dirt floor, providing ample space for storing most of the park's maintenance gear.

The upper floor of the barn is a spacious, cavernous area, with a few wide, long floorboards that are loose, revealing gaps that offer glimpses of the floor below. Hooks hang from the beams, and partial walls hint at sections that once served functional purposes in the barn's earlier days.

Access to the upper floor is via a high, grass-covered bank on the eastern side facing the park. Large sliding doors open to the interior, and an expansive covered porch on its second level was transformed a few years ago into an electrified stage for the park's entertainment events. The vast grassy field between the barn and the park's parking lot became an ideal area for concerts, car shows, or additional parking for other gatherings in the early years.

With permission of the cemetery board, the barn stage has hosted two fundraising concerts with audiences spreading out on the lawn, relaxing on chairs and enjoying picnics, creating a vibrant and community-centered atmosphere at the park.

Dean Phillips has also been a steadfast presence at the park. A Clinton resident since 2001, his backyard borders the park's south side, giving him a strong sense of connection to the area. During his career at First Energy as a utility distribution system and safety expert, Dean volunteered his time to assist with numerous park projects. Now retired, he spends his days with family, friends, and his greenhouse, while still finding time to pursue his various hobbies. His dedication to the park remains unwavering—he regularly mows and maintains the lawns and continues to assist John, Ken, and others whenever new projects arise.

"Hey, Dale, you want to help me build a pavilion? Know anything about that?" Ken asked, eager to start a new project on the property. Building a structure was part of the agreement with the cemetery board, and he decided that 2012 was the year to make it happen. Ken laid out a rectangle measuring thirty-two by fifty-six feet, dug deep holes at each corner, and the construction began. Dale Smith, another dedicated volunteer with some construction skills, helped set the posts. Dean assisted Ken and Dale in getting the roof up. The pavilion quickly became a hub for gatherings, housing picnic tables, and hosting Christmas events, with canvas walls to keep out the cold and rugs on the dirt floor. Finally, in 2014, a concrete floor was poured, giving it a more permanent feel.

"Ken and Dean roofing the pavilion-OVMP archives"

"I knew nothing at all about construction," Ken admitted. "I can't tell you how many mistakes I made and had to fix. At one point, the saw just stopped. I thought the electric went off and I realized I had cut through the cord. Oh, the number of electrical cords I ruined on Dean's saws—he could probably tell you exactly how many."

"Pavilion before the walls were built-OVMP archives"

    It wasn't until 2015, after the pavilion was fully enclosed and the interior finished, that it was officially named the Family of Heroes Hall. This marked a new opportunity to honor soldiers, as large granite tiles became a unique tribute on the structure's exterior. Chosen and designed by loved ones, the twelve-by-twelve-inch tiles, placed on the windowless east and north sides, feature laser-engraved, high-resolution photos of soldiers. Alongside these images are inspirational sayings and information about the military personnel being remembered or honored, creating a lasting tribute to their service.

CHAPTER FIVE

"Granite photo wall on the outside walls of the Family of Heroes Hall-photo credit Steve Wallis"

One tile holds a particularly special significance for thousands of people—not just family and friends, and not just Ohioans.

This tile honors Ashley Irene White, a remarkable young woman from Marlboro, Ohio, whose legacy has grown far beyond what she might have imagined following her tragic death in Afghanistan on October 22, 2011.

"Lt Ashley White at work-courtesy of the White family"

Ashley was an Army first lieutenant with the 230th Brigade Support Battalion, 30th Heavy Brigade Combat Team, North Carolina National Guard, based in Goldsboro, NC. She volunteered for the Cultural Support Team (CST), a groundbreaking all-female unit created to work alongside special operations forces. After completing her training, she was assigned to a Joint Special Operations Task Force in Kandahar. While not directly engaged in combat, Ashley and her CST colleagues operated near conflict zones, engaging with Afghan women—half of the population that U.S. soldiers were culturally unable to approach. The team's mission was to gather intelligence and crucial local information that could only be accessed through direct interactions with women.

Throughout her career, Ashley's dedication and professionalism shone brightly. She worked tirelessly to prove herself, displaying the competence, selflessness, and commitment that made her an ideal fit

Chapter Five

for the CST. By all accounts, she embodied the very best qualities of a soldier and a leader, leaving a profound and lasting impact on those who had the honor of serving alongside her.

This was no social work mission. Ashley worked alongside the Rangers in some of the most dangerous areas. She built vital relationships with local women, gathering crucial information that would have been inaccessible otherwise. Though she wasn't there to kick down doors, as she had confided to her brother Josh, Ashley was fully aware of the risks when she signed up. She took pride in being at the forefront of a pioneering initiative, understanding the significance of her role as a woman in this pathbreaking program.

A CST trainer, Captain Tara Matthews, captured the essence of their mission in a letter to the team: "Your presence here has been foretold by the generations of women that preceded us in military service to the nation, and you walk a path in advance of a more efficient and tested generation that will strive to follow you and carry us into the future."[3] Ashley and her team were true trailblazers, redefining what it meant to serve on the front lines.

Ashley had always been a quiet child; she was the reserved twin in contrast to her lively sister Brittany. "Sometimes we would have to turn around and make sure she was still with the family; she was so quiet," recalled her mother, Debbie White. Observant and sweet, Ashley would often lose track of her surroundings, like the time she stood watching a caterpillar crawl to the ceiling during gymnastics class. She shared a close bond with her sister and their older brother Josh, growing even closer as they all got older.

To the surprise of her family, especially Brittany, Ashley blossomed during her time at Kent State University. The once-quiet twin transformed into a confident and assertive young woman. "She became the alpha twin," her mom remarked. Ashley joined the Reserve Officers' Training Corps, or ROTC, and began to truly come into her own. She had been a cross-country runner in high school but excelled even further in college, becoming the first woman to make Kent State's Ranger ROTC team. She traveled with the team to compete against other colleges. Once an opposing team's coach was dismayed that a woman had outpaced his team's male runner. That was Ashley.

Though the Rangers were not always welcoming to female soldiers, Ashley quickly proved herself. Debbie recalled that Ashley's comrades initially gave her the nickname "Muffin"—a playful yet ironic moniker, given her blend of femininity and toughness. Despite her soft-spoken demeanor, Ashley was strong and relentless, impressing even the most skeptical. Her Ranger peers, intimidated by her dedication and fitness, often avoided the gym when she was working out, not wanting to be outdone. Over time, the Rangers came to recognize and respect her as one of their own, a sentiment that now endures as part of her legacy.

Ashley was tragically killed by an improvised explosive device on October 22, 2011. The device was part of a daisy chain—a series of linked IEDs designed to cause maximum damage. Two Rangers also lost their lives in the attack, and many others were injured. The loss sent shock waves through her CST team and the Rangers she served alongside, leaving them devastated by her passing.

Ashley had been married to Jason Stumpf, who was also in the military, for five months. Her mother, Debbie, still finds it impossible to return to the church where Ashley's funeral was held so soon after the joy of her wedding. Ashley had just celebrated her twenty-fourth birthday a few weeks before her death, and she had dreamed of returning home to be a wife, a mother, and to be surrounded by her loving family.

Chapter Five

"Happy days. The bride, Ashley White with her parents, Bob and Debbie, and her twin sister, Brittany, and brother, Josh-courtesy of the White family"

In an effort to protect her family, Ashley had downplayed the dangers of her assignment, which was reassuring to her parents. On that cool October morning, Debbie was baking cupcakes, and Bob, Ashley's father, was at work when the phone rang. Jason, her son-in-law, calling from his base out west, asked to speak to Bob. Debbie, not suspecting anything was wrong, gave him a hard time before finally telling him to call the shop where Bob was working.

Jason had been the first to receive the devastating news of Ashley's death, and he couldn't bear to tell Debbie while she was alone. Bob returned home to deliver the news, and the world as they knew it shattered.

Within hours, Army officers arrived at their home, but by then, friends and family had already gathered, filling the house with shock, grief, and attempts to console one another. The news of Ashley's death had already been broadcast on national television, compounding the surreal and overwhelming grief. Despite the heartbreaking circumstances, Debbie and Bob were grateful that Jason had been the one to call them first, softening what would have otherwise been a more harrowing notification. The loss of Ashley forever altered their family, and life would never be the same.

"She never wanted attention for herself," her mother said. Yet, Ashley White Stumpf's legacy has captured the attention of three U.S. presidents and their families, two of whom her family had the chance to meet. Her story has also reached book authors, film studios, screenwriters, a famous actress, as well as military leaders like Admiral William McRaven and Lt. Gen. John Mulholland. She is honored in women's military museums, Army museums, and has been posthumously awarded numerous medals and ribbons. Despite all this, Debbie believes that Ashley wouldn't have sought or cared about the accolades.

When Ashley earned her Combat Action Badge, her fellow soldiers only found out about it through other channels because she never mentioned it herself. When they approached her, asking, "Why didn't you tell us?" she simply responded, "It's not that big a deal." But it was a big deal—that was just Ashley.

This modest, determined young woman broke through barriers in the military, paving the way for others. Her story is powerfully captured in the book *Ashley's War: The Untold Story of a Team of Women Soldiers on the Special Ops Battlefield* by Gayle Tzemach Lemmon, where Captain Matthews's letter to Ashley's CST team is also quoted. Although a screenplay has been developed, the planned movie adaptation was put on hold due to the Covid pandemic. Still, Ashley's story—and the story of her fellow trailblazing women—awaits the opportunity to be shared on the big screen with someone brave enough to bring her and those women's courage and sacrifice to light.

Chapter Five

If Ashley had returned from Kandahar to receive the accolades she so deserved and someone had asked her, "Which honor would you like to be your legacy?" her mother, Debbie, is certain Ashley's answer would have been to name the villages in her honor.

Ashley's Houses and Ashley's Cottage are part of the New Beginnings Women Veterans Transition Homes, developed by Villagers For Veterans, an organization that would have been close to Ashley's heart. These all-female transition homes offer a safe and supportive environment where female veterans can transition back to civilian life. A HUD and VA (Departments of Housing and Veterans Affairs) study found that female veterans are more likely to experience homelessness than their male counterparts, and many do not feel comfortable or safe in traditional veteran facilities. These homes provide focused counseling, training, and a sense of camaraderie, offering a place of healing and growth. Ashley would have been immensely proud of this legacy.

Debbie White has attended and continues to participate in many ceremonies and events dedicated to her daughter's memory. Still, the struggle of grief often remains silent. For Gold Star parents, the loss encompasses not just a child but also the hopes, dreams, and future that will never come to pass. Public ceremonies can stir mixed emotions of pride and pain. Debbie thought she had heard everything there was to say about Ashley's impact, but one moment at the Military Women's Memorial in Arlington National Cemetery left a lasting impression.

After giving a speech, Debbie was approached by an elderly woman veteran dressed in a wool WWII uniform. Debbie shook her hand and said, "Thank you for your service." The woman firmly replied, "No! I want to thank you. Your daughter made what I did in the service mean so much more than it ever did."

That was Ashley—the White family's "muffin" with a core of steel.

Chapter Six

Friendship is the only cement that will ever hold the world together.

—Woodrow Wilson

2013–2014

Another wheelbarrow of fill dirt was dumped and shoveled up against the Reflecting Pond's granite wall. The volunteers had long since lost count of the number of loads. The back of the wall needed support, and shoveling was the only way to get it done. As they worked, an old red pickup truck with utility bins hanging off the sides and a gas-powered welder in the bed slowly passed them on the circle road. The driver nodded at the men, then drove on.

"That was Farmer. Why didn't he stop to chat as usual?" asked Dean, emptying his wheelbarrow.

"He'll be back," Ken said. "He just gave me that what-an-idiot look."

Within the hour, Farmer was back, this time with a front-end loader attached to his tractor—probably a self-built half-circuit hydraulic system, Dean thought, just like the one his own grandfather had put on his tractor. This would make short work of hauling dirt.

Farmer, known to the park volunteers as Farmer "MacGyver," had become a fixture at the park, bringing his farm machinery, hard work, and dry humor. In his seventies, he was the kind of guy who could fix anything. He had a knack for always finding a better way to do things. His family farm wasn't far, and one day he just showed up—then kept showing up. He usually had pliers, wrenches, and screwdrivers on hand, and if not, he'd head back to the farm to grab what was needed.

"I never knew his real name," Dean recalled. He often sat with Farmer, chatting about the world while they watched Ken work.

"Ken would come up with some odd ideas about how to do something and then just go for it, and Farmer would shake his head," Dean said, smiling. "Farmer and I would talk about how it wasn't going to work and how Ken was a dope for trying it that way. Oddly enough, it worked most of the time. But that didn't stop us from giving Ken a hard time. I really enjoyed old Farmer."

Farmer was just one of the many generous friends who supported the memorial park. The park couldn't have thrived without them. The local help never ceased to amaze the volunteers: the hands-on work, thoughtfulness, and donations of time, energy, equipment, and materials. But perhaps most memorable was the camaraderie and spirit these friends brought, making every effort feel like a true community endeavor.

Larry Props, owner of Props Masonry for forty-five years, was one of the dedicated friends of the memorial park. A Vietnam veteran, Larry returned home after his service to start his own company and raise his family. For a couple of decades, he also officiated youth and high school football. In whatever spare time he had, he made it a priority to help his fellow veterans at the memorial park.

Chapter Six

Larry put blocks around buildings and poured tons of concrete. "He was incredibly patient," Dean recalled, "when teaching the guys about stone veneer and grout. Whenever something needed to be moved, Larry would show up with his dump truck, always ready to lend a hand." Eighty percent of the concrete work at the park was done at cost by Larry, including the footers for the entire Ohio Vietnam wall, the pads for the helicopter, the monuments, and most of the concrete under the bricks.

Even during his battle with stomach cancer, Larry continued to volunteer, much to the concern of his wife and family. It was particularly distressing for them when he used what little energy he had to show up at the park after sessions of chemotherapy. Yet, Larry was resolute. "I understand that it's worrisome when I'm weak, but I can't just stay home, sit, and wait to die," he told the park volunteers.

Larry passed away in 2016 at the age of sixty-eight, after a three-year battle with cancer. He was laid to rest at the Ohio Western Reserve National Cemetery. In a final act of generosity, his family honored the OVMP by asking for memorial contributions to be made to the park. Today, a granite bench stands in his memory, commemorating his service in the Army from 1967 to 1971 and celebrating him as a cherished friend of the Ohio Veterans Memorial Park.

Not all deaths from major illnesses and cancer among Vietnam veterans are related to military service, but many are. Certain cancers, birth defects, and other health issues can often be traced back to exposure to Agent Orange, an herbicide used extensively during the Vietnam War. This chemical had various applications, but it was primarily used to defoliate dense jungle areas, clearing large swaths of vegetation to expose enemy hideouts, supply routes, and food sources.

Agent Orange was deployed over a period of about ten years, aimed at revealing hidden enemy shelters, supplies, and the Viet Cong themselves. The long-term health effects of this chemical were not fully understood at the time, but decades later, the damage has become tragically clear. The U.S. Department of Veterans Affairs now recognizes more than twenty presumptive conditions linked to Agent Orange exposure, burn pits, and other toxic exposures, making veterans eligible for treatment. Despite this, thousands of Vietnam veterans continue to suffer and die from illnesses connected to their exposure.[1]

August 10 marks the anniversary of the first time Agent Orange was sprayed in Vietnam. Every year on this date, orange candles are lit at the Vietnam Veterans Memorial wall in Washington, D.C., and other memorials across the country to observe Agent Orange Awareness Day. The use of this defoliant has left a painful legacy, acknowledged on several benches at the park that commemorate veterans whose deaths were attributed to the effects of Agent Orange.

Chapter Six

"Sgt. Johnnie Downs behind his family bench-OVMP archives"

Army Sergeant First Class Johnnie R. Downs is a steadfast supporter of the park. He retired from the military in 2006 after serving for "32 years, 6 months, 24 days, 7 hours, and 23 seconds," he proudly recounted.[2] Throughout his career, he served in Vietnam, Desert Storm, the Cold War, and the War on Terrorism. A proud Buffalo Soldier, Johnnie takes every opportunity to highlight and recognize the contributions of African American and Native American military personnel.

Johnnie's brother Herman Downs was born in Akron, Ohio, in 1947, the third of five children. After finishing high school, Herman followed in Johnnie's footsteps and enlisted in the military, volunteering as a Marine to serve in Vietnam. Both brothers were stationed in

Vietnam from 1966 to 1967. For Herman, the war would mark the beginning of a lifelong struggle.

Shortly after his return home, Herman began showing signs of post-traumatic stress disorder (PTSD), and it became evident he was struggling to adjust to civilian life. At the age of thirty-eight, he was diagnosed with cancer, a direct result of his exposure to Agent Orange during his service. The illness was devastating, affecting his face and head and ultimately leading to the removal of his tongue. Over time, the cancer disfigured Herman's face, causing immense suffering for him and his family. Herman passed away on June 5, 1990, leaving behind a family deeply scarred by his ordeal.

In memory of his brother, Johnnie worked tirelessly to have Herman honored through the Vietnam Veterans Memorial Fund's In Memory Program. Each year, Johnnie attends the In Memory Weekend Ceremony in front of the Vietnam Veterans Memorial in Washington, D.C., where he speaks about Herman's life and legacy.

At the 2017 ceremony, Johnnie shared, "My heroes don't dribble a basketball; they don't throw a football. My heroes are Vietnam veterans and the people that are on this wall today."

From the outset, Delmer believed the park's walkways would serve to honor all military dead from all wars, though he still wanted the organization to retain "Vietnam" in its name. The bricks available for purchase at the park were designed to honor soldiers from any war and from across the United States, but bricks directly in front of the Vietnam wall were specifically for those who served in Vietnam. This distinction led to some controversy.

There were debates over who qualified for a brick placement in front of the wall. Questions arose about those who served during the Vietnam era but were stationed stateside or in other locations like

Chapter Six

Germany. Did they deserve a spot near the wall, or should those spaces be reserved solely for combat veterans? These discussions sparked disagreements, and feeling that their loved ones deserved the honor, some were unhappy when the bricks they purchased were not placed in front of the wall.

"Stacks of bricks to be laid in walkways-OVMP archives"

The initial delivery of sixteen thousand red bricks marked the beginning of a significant project at the park. Stacks upon stacks were unloaded, the first of many deliveries needed to pave the extensive walkways. Although the limestone base was already laid and firm, stretching from the main walk to the center of the wall, no volunteer had the initial skills to tackle the task of paving the hundreds of feet of brick paths. Stakes and strings outlined the walkways, which were dug six to eight inches deep and slightly sloped to allow for proper drainage.

Over time, a few volunteers learned the technique and gradually took on the project, laying the bricks month by month. Around the wall itself, they installed a wide swath of stamped concrete, which served as a base for benches, with the bricks meeting up seamlessly to the concrete edges. The work began at the slope from the parking lot, working downward toward the wall, with paths leading to the six flagpoles that represented the different branches of the military.

As the volunteers worked, often on their knees, visitors passed by, sometimes pausing to observe or ask questions. Motorcycle groups of veterans stopped, curious about the effort. When asked what they were doing, it gave the volunteers an opportunity to explain, "You know, we are all volunteers doing this." The hope was that those who showed interest might offer to lend a hand or perhaps return later with friends to assist. Unfortunately, few did.

The people who did step up were often local neighbors or the families of the volunteers. On one occasion, an elderly woman joined Ken as he worked on placing and leveling bricks. She would walk to the pile, retrieve a brick, and bring it back to him.

"I picked up and placed four bricks for every one she handed me," Ken recalled, "but I acted like I couldn't do it without her. I appreciated her help. It was nice to have people who cared."

A couple, Kitty Phillips Williams and Richard Williams, were both on the committee and key volunteers in the laying of the bricks. "They showed up and worked so hard, both of them, to get the walkways done. They were amazing," both Chuck and Ken remembered.

Back in 2009, few volunteers had the technical skills on the computer to create the materials needed to rally community support. One man, however, stood out: Steve Cripple.

Chapter Six

Steve wasn't always out digging trenches or moving dirt; his work was in the "indoor trenches," where he put in just as much effort. He created colorful, informative brochures, flyers, and announcements for fundraising events. His technical expertise was invaluable, especially in developing the park's website. A genius with a camera and computer, and an artist in his own right, Steve did something truly powerful for volunteerism—he brought his family into the fold.

"Veronica and Steve Cripple-courtesy of the Cripple family"

Stephen D. Cripple was deeply committed to his family, veterans, and the OVMP. When he and his wife, Veronica, decided to move their family from an apartment to a house with a yard, one of their key criteria was proximity to the park. They found the perfect home, and Veronica still lives there today. "We were a big part of the park," she reflected, "and it was a big part of us for a good ten years. It meant so much to us."

Neither Steve nor Veronica were veterans, but they both dedicated enormous time and energy to the park in those early days, showing up, as true friends do, to every event. Their children naturally became involved, too, and even provided the veteran connection for the family. Their daughter Danielle—known as Katie, short for her middle name Kathleen—joined the Army and later married a Marine. Both have since come home, and Chris, Katie's husband, is now in the Air Force and serves in the Akron police department. They have four children who keep the family busy. Steve and Veronica's son Steven also got involved in park projects over the years and eventually became a board member, following in his parents' footsteps.

"Steve and I always felt a special affinity for veterans. Steve, especially, held them all close to his heart. We once made business cards on our own with the OVMP info on one side and 'thank you for your service!' on the other. We'd give them to our favorite waitress Michele Barker at a restaurant where we often had lunch. Michele learned the routine."

The routine was Veronica and Steve would discreetly point out a suspected veteran dining nearby. Michele would, instead of presenting the bill, give the chosen veteran the card. Then she would tell them their meal had been paid for anonymously by someone who was thankful for their service.

"We got everything from tears to having our own meal paid for once," Veronica recalled. "We had such fun doing it. And the veterans would often come to the park later. It delighted Steve. It was a good thing!"

Chapter Six

Steve and Veronica were especially invested in supporting Gold Star Mothers. "When they came to the park, we paid special attention to them," Veronica said. She got to know many of these mothers well. On one occasion, she found a grieving mother sobbing on the other side of the wall before a ceremony. "It was pouring rain, a real blowing storm. I went to her side, and she managed to tell me that she was there to place a brick for her son, as she had chosen to do."

At that time, families had the option to personally place their loved one's brick rather than having a volunteer do it. This Gold Star mother was heartbroken to find that the brick had been laid before she arrived. Veronica found Steve, who immediately went out into the storm, retrieved the brick, and brought it back. The ceremony continued, and the mother was able to lay her son's brick herself.

The emotions of Gold Star parents—pride and sorrow intertwined—are profound, especially without the closure of a goodbye to their child. It is a complex and delicate balance, where the recognition of their child's service brings both comfort and feelings of isolation. These parents need tender care.

When her daughter returned safely from combat in Afghanistan, Veronica was, of course, immensely relieved. "At the same time, it was hard to face my friends, the Gold Star Mothers who had lost their children."

Her fears, Veronica discovered, were unfounded. When Katie came home, the Gold Star Mothers surrounded her with joy and love. "Never be sorry for saying how happy you are to have her home," one mother told her. "We are happy that she is home too."

Steve lost his battle with cancer in 2022 at the age of fifty. Veronica lost the love of her life, and their children lost a devoted dad and grandfather. The OVMP lost a true friend, and veterans across the country lost a dedicated supporter.

Another staunch supporter of the OVMP is Allen Knack, who served as the mayor of Clinton from 2013 to 2020.

"When I first became mayor," he recalled, "I stopped by the park when I saw a lone car there. I wanted to introduce myself. I found a couple seated on a bench, gazing at the wall. They said they were there to see their son and talk to him. I sat with them, and together, I shared their tears."

That poignant moment solidified Al's commitment to the park, and he made it a priority throughout his time as mayor. "Whatever I can do, I'm there!" Al Knack vowed to himself. For the next eight years he stood by that promise.

As a businessman, Al knew how to leverage relationships and goodwill. Over the years, he had built connections by helping others, and he wasn't shy about calling in favors when needed. He believed that if people were aware of the veterans' needs at the park and were in a position to help, they would step up.

One memorable example of his determination involved trying to get direction signs for the OVMP on a nearby highway. However, a portion of the highway was in a different county, and the officials there were resistant, insisting they weren't responsible for promoting "attractions" outside their jurisdiction.

"I was so mad," Al recalled. But he didn't let frustration get the best of him. Instead, he calmly called them back and made his case: "This is the deal. I won't go to the TV, radio stations, newspapers, or social media to tell them you refuse to put up a sign to the Ohio Veterans Memorial Park if you agree to put up the sign."

Chapter Six

His efforts spurred lobbying by Randy Dunbar, a member of American Legion Post 221, who led a petition campaign involving veteran groups. With their support, they appealed to a state legislator who in turn contacted the Ohio Department of Transportation. By Veterans Day in 2012, direction signs to the park were posted on all major highways.

"We all wanted to help the park succeed," Al said. There was never an inappropriate influence, only trust and personal connection. Al continues to promote the park wherever he and his wife, Carol, travel across the country.

The park holds a special place in their hearts, so much so that Al and Carol have made arrangements to be laid to rest there. Behind the park, near the circle road, stands a small columbarium—a modern crypt with niches for cremated remains. It belongs to the cemetery, and the two have reserved their spots, with Al saying, "We love it in the park and can't think of anywhere we would rather rest."

At the park, special events continued to bring people together in remembrance. On September 11, 2013, a service was held to place a black granite marker commemorating the lives lost during the deadly attacks in Benghazi, Libya, a year earlier. The assaults on the U.S. diplomatic and CIA compounds resulted in the deaths of four Americans: U.S. ambassador to Libya, Chris Stevens; Sean Smith, a foreign service worker; and two Navy SEALs, Tyrone Woods and Glen Doherty.[3]

Though the Navy SEALs were not Ohioans, the park committee felt strongly that their service and sacrifice should be honored. During the ceremony, the marker was laid in the OVMP, with the help of military personnel from the Navy and Marine recruiting offices in Canton.

The attacks in Benghazi had deeply impacted the nation, and the event at the park served as a meaningful gesture of respect. A number of local residents and OVMP volunteers gathered to witness the ceremony. Don was among those present. He said it brought tears to his eyes to see the two Navy SEALs honored in this way, remarking, "This is what the park is about."

Summit Memorials Inc. served as a central hub for much of the park's communication during its first couple of years. Their business phone number even doubled as the OVMP's contact, as Summit was open during business hours with someone always available to answer calls—a necessity since the park had no indoor facilities or dedicated phone line at the time. Barbara Freeman, a former schoolteacher who worked as the secretary at Ken's shop, became the go-to coordinator for much of the fundraising and brick sales. "I loved every minute of it," she recalled. "I was very organized, and no bricks were lost or misspelled on my watch. I cared about these veteran families. I had veterans in my family as well."

Barbara's personal connection to the cause led her to honor an uncle she had never met but had heard many stories about—her father's only sibling, Stephen Szerecz. He was a U.S. Army Ranger in the 5th Battalion, one of the units involved in the invasion of Omaha Beach during World War II. Known for leading the charge, the Rangers broke through the seawall and barbed wire, advancing up and over German pillboxes. Omaha Beach was one of five key sectors of the amphibious-assault component of Operation Overlord on D-Day, June 6, 1944.

Technician Fifth Grade Stephen Szerecz was killed in action on that historic day. He is buried in the Normandy American Cemetery and Memorial in France, a site covering 172.5 acres that contains the graves of 9,389 American military dead.[4]

Chapter Six

Stephen was one of two soldiers from the congregation of the Sacred Heart Church on Grant Street in Akron who were honored with sacred bronze founts. After the church was closed, like many Roman Catholic parishes in recent decades, Barbara managed to retrieve her uncle's bronze memorial. Her husband later mounted it on the back porch of their house, where it remains a cherished tribute to this day.

Barbara decided to honor her uncle Stephen Szerecz in a profound and lasting way by commissioning a monument for the OVMP. It became the first Purple Heart monument known to be placed in a U.S. veterans memorial park. The monument was designed, built, and installed by her boss, Ken. The Purple Heart, one of the most recognized symbols of military sacrifice, is awarded to service members who have been wounded or have lost their lives in service to the nation.

"Ceremony at the Purple Heart monument-photo credit Steve Wallis"

"Reflection of Barbara Freeman reflected in the monument dedicated to her uncle" -OVMP archives"

The Purple Heart awarded to Stephen's family after his death is part of a legacy that dates back to its origins as the oldest military decoration still in use today. It is also the first American award made available to the common soldier. General George Washington established it as the Badge of Military Merit on August 7, 1782. He wrote: "The General ever desirous to cherish virtuous ambition in his soldiers as well as foster and encourage every species of military merit, directs that whenever any singularly military action is performed, the author of it shall be permitted to wear on his facings, over his left breast, the figure of a heart in purple cloth or silk edged in narrow lace or binding . . . The road to glory in a patriot army and a free country is thus open to all."

Chapter Six

Given for wounds or death in combat, the Purple Heart led to the formation of the Military Order of the Purple Heart in 1932, dedicated to the protection and mutual interest of all recipients. It remains the only veterans' service organization composed solely of combat veterans. August 7 is now recognized as National Purple Heart Day in honor of Washington's original directive.[5]

The monument at the OVMP bears this history, engraved in granite next to an oversized representation of the Purple Heart medal, carved into the stone and painted a striking purple and gold. At its center is a relief of George Washington's profile. It stands as a tribute to bravery, valor, and selfless dedication. Barbara's intention was for the Purple Heart Memorial to serve as a reminder of sacrifice and to inspire gratitude for soldiers like Stephen of their unwavering commitment to freedom and justice. Stephen Szerecz's name, rank, and date of death are engraved on the back of the monument. The OVMP Purple Heart Memorial was dedicated on June 1, 2013.

In the following months and years, Barbara continued her role, handling orders for monuments and bricks for the park. One day, she received a call from a woman who wanted to order a brick for a veteran. The woman mentioned she had visited the park and admired the beauty of the Purple Heart monument. Barbara shared that her family had proudly dedicated it to her uncle who had died on D-Day. The woman responded appreciatively but remarked that the man in the center of the gold heart looked "a little too much like George Washington."

Barbara later laughed about the comment, amused by the thought that the woman might have expected the image to represent her Uncle Stephen.

In 2013, the POW/MIA Reflecting Pond and Wall were completed, adding a solemn and striking feature to the OVMP. The black granite wall, fifty feet wide, was designed to echo the tapering lines of the Vietnam Memorial in Washington, D.C., with its height descending from an eight-foot peak at the center to just one foot at each end.

"Careful installation of the granite panels at the POW pond -OVMP archives"

The installation of the granite panels involved some tense and challenging moments. During the process, there were harrowing incidents where the crane, overextended, caused a granite slab to topple, narrowly missing Ken's leg. To position each panel securely, the team used a technique involving dry ice. A belt was wrapped around the granite to lift it into place, and once set on the foundation, a bed of dry ice was used to allow the belt to slip out easily. As the dry ice evaporated, it left no water behind, ensuring the panel settled smoothly. However, under one panel, the dry ice had been unevenly distributed, causing the granite to slip off the foundation as it evaporated. Thankfully, no one was hurt, and the team was able to reposition the panel correctly.

Chapter Six

When finished, the Reflecting Pond and Wall created a beautiful and serene tribute. The black granite wall stood starkly against the fifty feet of still, black water, with the bright, flickering eternal flame adding a vivid contrast. Surrounding the pond were lush flowers and grasses, with a spacious sitting area dotted with benches, offering visitors a place for reflection and peace accompanied by the calming sounds of a cascading waterfall. Near the sitting area, a large piece of black granite—originally intended for the Ohio Vietnam Wall—was repurposed as a marker and engraved with the history of the POW/MIA flag. Above this tranquil scene, the POW/MIA flag flew proudly, a symbol of remembrance and hope. The wall of polished black granite at the pond not only reflected the sky and flame but also mirrored the visitor gazing across the pond, reinforcing the poignant message: Until They All Come Home.

"Cascading waterfalls to the POW pond-OVMP archives"

The dedication ceremony for the completed pond and reflecting wall took place on November 21, 2013. Chaplain James Scalf, a retired Navy officer, delivered the opening prayer and benediction, setting a tone of reverence and reflection for all those gathered.

Each year, on the first Saturday of August, a small but powerful scene is set by the pond at the POW/MIA Reflection Pond and Eternal

Flame. A single table and chair stand in the grass, with a white tablecloth, a lit candle, a Bible, an inverted wine glass, and a single red rose in a vase tied with a yellow ribbon. On the table, there is also an empty plate with a lemon wedge and a pinch of salt. Each of these items carries symbolic meaning, representing the absence and sacrifice of missing soldiers. This is the Missing Man Table, the poignant centerpiece of an annual ceremony dedicated to remembering and honoring POW/MIA service members.[6]

"Missing Man Table at the dedication of the POW pond-photo credit Chuck Nicholas"

The ceremony, performed by the American Legion Riders, is a solemn tribute to all U.S. soldiers who were prisoners of war or are still

Chapter Six

missing in action. This year (2024), the names of 127 recovered U.S. service members and their military branches were read aloud, each followed by the toll of a bell. These names included soldiers who served in World War II, the Korean War, and the Vietnam War. For each name, a volunteer placed a long-stemmed red rose on a table beside the Missing Man Table. Volunteers with military backgrounds offered a salute, while others gave a bow or nod of respect. The dignified and heartfelt event served as a reminder of the ongoing commitment to honoring those who have endured captivity and those who have yet to return home.

The numbers underscore the gravity of this issue: Across all conflicts since World War I, more than 100,000 U.S. service members remain unaccounted for. Over 81,000 Americans are still missing from World War II, the Korean War, the Cold War, and the Vietnam War.[7] The Defense POW/MIA Accounting Agency, a part of the U.S. Department of Defense, is dedicated to locating, recovering, and identifying the remains of these missing service members.[8] Through painstaking recovery and identification efforts, the DPAA aims to bring closure to families who have waited years, and sometimes decades, to bring their loved ones home.

The pressure to remain "the strong one" is a profound challenge for fathers who lose a son or daughter during military service. While Gold Star Mothers have long been acknowledged and supported, fathers often face an invisible struggle, left out of the public narrative and sometimes unacknowledged in ceremonies. Many Gold Star fathers wrestle with feelings of guilt over having encouraged or supported their child's decision to serve, along with a sense of failure as the family's protector. This can deeply complicate their grieving process.

Recognizing this need, a Gold Star father suggested a statue be created to join the existing *Gold Star Mother* statue at the park. On

May 17, 2014, the fifth anniversary of the Vietnam Wall dedication, the *Gold Star Father* statue was unveiled and positioned on the east side of the wall. Facing the *Gold Star Mother* statue through the wall, they stand eight and a half feet tall, symbolically seeing one another across the divide. Both statues hold a flag close to their granite bodies, a poignant gesture of pride and loss.

"Gold Star Father statue-photo credit Steve Wallis"

This statue, believed to be the first of its kind in the country, was inspired by Scott Warner of Canton, Ohio. Warner—who wrote a memoir titled *Gold Star Father* about the loss of his son Marine Private Heath Warner, who was killed in Iraq in 2006—said of the statue, "It tells our story." Speaking to the *Akron Beacon Journal* before the dedication, he shared, "When you receive that flag in your arms and all those feelings—pain, honor, and sadness—come together at one point, that is the story of the statue. It is all about honor and love."⁹

The Gold Star Father monument was carved by Ken at Summit Memorials, designed to mirror the existing *Gold Star Mother* statue. Its base is inscribed with a poem by Mansfield, Ohio, poet Kay A. McNaul, which reads in part:

His child grown and gone to war,
Then the call, 'Home no more.'
The memories of so many years,
Mingle with happy times and tears.
Your child in heaven safe from harm
Behold the final, fourteenth fold
As the Flag gently rests
In a proud father's folded arms.

The day of the dedication was marked by rain, reflecting the somber mood. Three Gold Star fathers—Steven Blackwell, who lost his son Justin; Tom Seesan, who lost his son Aaron; and Scott Warner, who lost his son Heath—spoke at the ceremony. Afterward, red, white, and blue balloons were released into the sky. Kay McNaul, present at the event, addressed the group of parents after reading her poem. Looking at their sorrowful faces, she remarked that the rain was like the tears they had shed for their lost children. In a moment of serendipity, a beam of sunlight broke through the clouds, illuminating the statue. She gently added, "It is a blessing of God, this *Gold Star Father* statue."

Also on the fifth anniversary of the Ohio Vietnam dedication, a bench funded by the Military Order of the Purple Heart, Chapter 699, was unveiled near the Purple Heart monument. It honors Ohio recipients of the medal, with their names engraved as a tribute to their bravery and sacrifice. This addition reflected the park committee's continued efforts to expand and enhance the memorial, ensuring it remains a focal point of community remembrance and respect. Through these initiatives, the committee has kept the park's mission alive in the hearts and minds of the local community.

"The portion of the Purple Heart Monument fashioned like the heart-shaped medal with the profile of George Washington-OVMP archives"

The Family of Heroes Hall had gradually become a central gathering place for volunteers and community members. It is open for the public to use year-round for memorial and military services, meetings, and events. The hall can comfortably seat fifty to sixty people with tables or over a hundred with chairs alone. Over the years, it had also evolved into an educational site, displaying military information and memorabilia contributed by staff and visitors. The park has even

Chapter Six

hosted a military wedding, with the Family of Heroes Hall serving as the perfect space for the reception.

One of the hall's most distinctive features is the Heroes Cross, a striking element in the center of the ceiling. A section is cut out in the shape of a cross, and from it hangs thousands of dog tags, each suspended on a six-inch chain from a cup hook, creating a stunning visual tribute.

Dog tags are used in the military for simple identification, primarily to recognize soldiers in case of a casualty. Each tag contains essential information such as the soldier's name, rank, serial number, blood type, inoculation history, and religion. The tradition is to wear two identical tags, ensuring one remains with the soldier if the other is removed. Due to their resemblance to animal ID tags, they are often referred to as "dog tags."

"32,768 dog tags representing Ohio soldiers KIA since WWII hanging from hooks in the Family Hall of Heroes- OVMP archives"

The creation of the Heroes Cross was a community effort. Volunteers organized contests for groups who participated in Dog-Tag Day, where teams competed to screw in cup hooks on predrilled plywood panels, prepared meticulously by Ken and Dean. The hooked wooden panels were then fixed to the ceiling within the cross-shaped cutout. Over three weekends, thousands of dog tags were taken to the Louis Stokes Cleveland VA Medical Center, where veteran patients helped assemble the chains and tags.

"Hero's Cross in the Family of Heroes Hall-photo credit Steve Wallis"

To install the display, volunteers used scaffolding to hang the dog tags from the ceiling hooks. The final result was eight panels with a total of 32,768 hanging tags. The cross is mirrored on the floor below with glossy black tiles, creating a reflective and poignant image. The number of dog tags represents the Ohio soldiers who were killed in action (KIA) since World War II, serving as a powerful testament to the community's dedication and honoring the sacrifice of its heroes.

Farmer's hydraulic line had broken on his front-loader tractor bucket while he was helping with the fill dirt. Ken recalled feeling bad about it, "When I get off work tomorrow, I will come to your barn and help you repair it."

Chapter Six

In his typical gruff, dry manner, Farmer responded, "How much do I know about tombstones? You want me coming to your work helping you?" Ken understood that as a firm no.

Early the next morning, Ken received an unexpected call from the mayor, Al Knack. "Can you come over right away? Farmer died last night." The police had notified Al that a village resident had passed away, and he was deeply saddened to learn it was Farmer. Ken was shocked, unable to comprehend what had happened.

It turned out that the evening before, Farmer had propped up the front-loader bucket still attached to the tractor, using a makeshift wooden jack to brace it. While he was underneath, the bucket collapsed, crushing him. He was alone outside the barn, and no one found him until much later.

Farmer's confused and grieving brothers couldn't understand why he had been fixing the tractor; as far as they knew, it had been working fine. Ken was able to explain the hydraulic issue from the day before and how Farmer had been trying to repair it. "I felt like it was my fault, and I kinda still do," Ken lamented. "If only the hydraulics hadn't broken while he was helping us. If only he had let me come help him fix it . . . if only . . ."

Chapter Seven

We giving all gained all
Neither lament us nor praise.
Only in all things recall,
It is Fear, not Death that slays.

—Rudyard Kipling, *Epitaphs of the War*

2015–2016

Gary Kindig walks the brick pathways nearly every day, carefully noting any weeds, bits of litter, or the occasional cigarette butt. He moves toward the central hub of the park, where walkways converge like spokes of a wheel, leading to a set of flagpoles flying the flags of different military branches. Eight black granite memorial benches are positioned around this entrance area of the park.

Gary stops, turns, and salutes one bench, pausing thoughtfully before moving on. This bench holds a special place in his heart. It memorializes a young man who was dear to him. At nineteen, Burt Everett Miller, known as Rusty to his family, is a Marine. Once a Marine, always a Marine—even in death, states Gary. An All-American young man, he graduated from Manchester High School in 1966, not far from the park. Gary, now in 2024 the president of the park committee, went to school with Rusty, knew him well, and considered him a close friend.

"Great guy, great friend," he recalled. Both Gary and Rusty served in Vietnam in 1968, but only Gary came home.

The loss of Rusty, like so many other young men and women, underscores the profound cost of war. The names etched on the wall, engraved on the benches, and set into the bricks represent not just the individuals but also the loss of futures, of potential lives that could have been long and fulfilling. This tragedy resonates deeply with families, communities, and society as a whole.

Jean Miller, now ninety-six, has spent fifty-six years without her son Rusty. Recently, she fondly recalled memories of him as a child, like the time he licked cake batter out of a bowl, getting chocolate all over his face. "I can still see it," she laughed. "And then I think of him out in the bush in Vietnam, just as he described in his letters. He once apologized for complaining about how stiff the sheets were at home after I had just changed them. I dried them outside on the line. He said he'd give anything for one of those clean sheets in Vietnam!" A knowing smile crossed her face as she remembered. Rusty was ornery, caring, and full of fun.

His sisters recounted a story about the time the women in the family left him to babysit two little ones while they went shopping. Although Jean never voiced her concerns about his babysitting skills, somehow Rusty sensed them. When they returned, they found the children safely in their playpens, and Rusty had staged a playful scene, complete with fake wounds on himself, a head bandaged and smeared with ketchup to look like blood, humorously showing the "pain" of his babysitting efforts.

Chapter Seven

"Sisters Darla, Billie and Rusty's mother, Jean-OVMP archives"

Jean and Bob, Rusty's father who passed away in 2018, were not initially told the full details of their son's death—only that he had died. Despite the heartbreaking news, Jean and her daughters were deeply touched by the outpouring of support from their community. "I had heard about the abuse young soldiers were facing when they returned, but we saw none of it," Jean said. "That's not how our friends felt. I've never felt so much love."

"Our house was never empty, and the community has never forgotten him," agreed Billie, one of Rusty's sisters. He had two sisters, Darla and Billie, and a younger brother, Blair. The family wasn't informed of the details of Rusty's death until 2002, decades after their world was first shattered. Their grief was reignited when Mike Murphy, the hospital corpsman who had been with Rusty in his final moments, managed to find the family after years of searching.

"Dad wanted to know everything, every detail, when Mike first called," Billie said. "But Mom was under a lot of stress, caring for her own ailing mother at the time."

"The information was difficult for both of them," Darla added. "It brought everything back—the pain and the memories. It was so good to talk about Rusty, but it also meant grieving deeply all over again."

Rusty and Mike were in the same platoon in the jungles—the 1st Platoon of Lima Company, 3rd Battalion, 5th Marine Regiment, 1st Marine Division. Rusty carried an M60 machine gun. He was a big guy at six feet, five inches.

"Mike said Rusty were very protective of the men with him," stated Billie.

Darla added, "Yes, if anyone had an issue it was always Rusty who would ask if they were OK."

Rusty was willing to use his M60 when necessary, and he often did so to protect his fellow soldiers. During one firefight, he covered Mike Murphy, firing to shield the medic as he dragged wounded men to safety. Mike told the family that they had lost many friends, and the toll was heavy. It made him wary of forming close bonds, but he couldn't help but love Rusty and his infectious grin. As men were lost and new recruits joined the platoon, Rusty made a point of looking out for the newcomers. Even after being hospitalized with pneumonia, he returned to his unit during the monsoon season in November 1968.

According to a December 2004 article in *Vietnam Magazine*,[1] Rusty, Mike, and another Marine machine gunner were in the jungle, navigating through a maze of booby traps and ambushes, when a single grenade landed on Rusty's chest. He was in a near-reclining position, climbing awkwardly, when the grenade rolled between his gun and his body. Mike told the family that Rusty looked directly at him. Mike

Chapter Seven

felt that Rusty realized there was no way to throw the grenade without putting everyone in danger. In that moment, he made the decision to shield it with his own body. Mike saw him intentionally bend over the grenade. The explosion spared his comrades, but it didn't kill Rusty immediately. Mike managed to speak with him briefly, and Rusty conveyed that he knew he was heading to a better place. His parents were comforted by this.

As heartbreaking as it was for the family to learn how their son died, it also brought them peace to know the extent of his bravery. They understood that Rusty had found his own peace, secure in who he was and where he was going.

After his death, two letters from Rusty were delivered to his family. In them, he wrote of Vietnam as a "Garden of Eden gone wrong" and expressed his steadfast faith in God. He urged his parents to tell "the girls never to hate" and wrote, "If you ever want to get close to God, then come to Vietnam."

His helmet was sent home, on its cover he'd inscribed a simple, powerful message: "It's just you and me, right, God?"

Gary returned home from duty just days before he received the news of Rusty's death. "I wanted to leave Vietnam far behind me," he said, "and then I heard that news. I was devastated. I felt so guilty. Why did I make it home and he didn't?"

For many soldiers, coming back was not the relief they had hoped for. Facing the families of fallen brothers-in-arms was painfully difficult, and returning troops were often met with disdain due to the unpopularity of the war. Survivor's guilt weighed heavily on them, intensifying the burden of traumatic memories from the battlefield. The combination of these factors led to widespread struggles with drug and alcohol addiction, depression, PTSD, and even suicide. Sadly, these issues were not unique to Vietnam; they continued to affect veterans of later conflicts as well.

Master Sergeant Ron Hetrick served with the Ohio National Guard and was deployed to Iraq during Desert Storm in 1990. As part of a team of engineers, his mission was to dismantle explosives left by the enemy. After five months he returned home, but his experiences left him with post-traumatic stress and depression. One of the most haunting aspects of his service was witnessing acts of brutality and questioning how his own military could sometimes be as culpable as the enemy from these inhumane actions.

Since coming home, Ron has lost eight friends from the Ohio National Guard to suicide, while another fellow soldier survived an attempt and is grateful to be alive. Many veterans, like Ron, longed to return to a sense of normalcy and to fit back in once they were home, but for some, that adjustment remained painfully out of reach.

For many Vietnam veterans, the Ohio Veterans Memorial Park has become a place of healing. This was certainly true for Gary. When he began volunteering at the park mowing lawns, he saw an opportunity to honor his friend Rusty Miller with a memorial bench. Gary believed this would be a significant step in his own journey of coping, as well as a source of comfort for Rusty's family. He started his campaign with one hundred dollars from a friend who shared his vision. Determined, Gary reached out to friends and high school classmates, quickly raising $4,000 for the bench within weeks. Even he was surprised by the success of the campaign.

For the dedication, Gary was determined to make it special, insisting that nothing less than a Marine Corps Color Guard would do. After much effort, he petitioned the Pentagon, and just two weeks before the event, his request was granted.

CHAPTER SEVEN

"The dedication of the bench was wonderful," Darla recalled. "It meant so much to Mom and Dad. To all of us." Rusty was properly honored, and Gary paid him tribute.

The following year, the Miller family surprised Gary by purchasing an honorary bench in Gary's name. His wife worked alongside the Miller family and Ken to organize the surprise, which was presented to him during a ceremony that was already planned to honor three local soldiers from their high school. "I was so honored," Gary said. "That family treated me like a son. Like the son they lost." Rusty's mother had continued to honor other soldiers as well, writing kind letters to the mothers of Vietnam War soldiers whose obituaries she came across over the years.

In a touching gesture, a small utility vehicle, a Cushman Truckster, bearing Rusty's name and Marine title, was presented during Manchester High School's fiftieth high school reunion at the Family of Heroes Hall. It was reconditioned and rebuilt from two Trucksters by Dave Godwin and his brother Ray as a tribute to Rusty.

"Rusty Miller's bench-OVMP archives"

In 2017, Gary took another step to memorialize Rusty by petitioning the state to name a section of Ohio State Route 93 through the Manchester area, now New Franklin, as the "Vietnam USMC PFC Burt 'Rusty' Miller Memorial Highway." This required the proposal to be introduced as a house bill to the Ohio General Assembly, and once approved, the commemorative signage was placed along the highway.[2]

Don Maurer, mentioned previously as one of the early dedicated supporters of the Ohio Veterans Memorial Park, remained committed for years, taking on some of the most demanding and tedious tasks. "I just did what needed to be done," he said, summing up his no-nonsense approach. He personally laid thousands of bricks in the walkways and played a key role in numerous projects: the arrival of the Cobra helicopter, the excavation of the POW/MIA pond, and the display of the tank.

Don had warm memories of Larry Props and Farmer MacGyver but not such fond memories of Chelle Rossi. Challenges came working so closely with her on such ambitious endeavors.

Despite the ups and downs, Don's dedication to the park and his fellow veterans never wavered, leaving a lasting mark on the memorial and those who visit it. Many of Don Maurer's memories of working at the Ohio Veterans Memorial Park are filled with camaraderie spent alongside fellow volunteers and veterans.

His connection to service runs deep; he was a Marine Honor Guard in Washington, D.C., during the 1960s, present during the riots, and at Bobby Kennedy's funeral. In 1968, his high-security clearance led to a critical assignment—delivering top secret mail between battlegrounds in Vietnam as part of Marine Air in the 1st Marine Air Wing. His commanding officer instructed him that if his helicopter was ever shot down, he was to "blow up" the mail with a grenade. Flying up and down the coast in a CH-46 helicopter, Don managed to avoid being shot down but endured the constant threat of danger, especially in Da Nang, where "rockets would bomb us every morning at 3 a.m.!"

He returned home in 1969 and continued to serve in the Marines until 1971. After his military career, Don retired from the Ohio Department of Transportation at the age of sixty-one. Although he now faces health issues related to Agent Orange exposure, he remains active with a new passion: building military models.

"I build helicopters, action dioramas, and all kinds of things," Don said. "I really enjoy it, and many of the things I've built are on display in museums locally, in Washington, D.C., and even in Okinawa."

Don has also made significant contributions to the park's collection. After his friend Gary Vardon passed away, Gary's widow donated a Deuce-and-a-Half military truck to Don and the park. The truck, now fully operational, has become a fixture in local patriotic parades. Capable of carrying two and a half tons of cargo off road or five tons on highways, the Deuce-and-a-Half rests on a concrete pad next to the Cobra helicopter, symbolizing the dedication of those who continue to honor their fellow servicemen and women.

"Don Maurer in dress uniform for a park event-OVMP archives"

Tony Rubino often visited the park, walking along the brick pathways for his health. One day, he met Ken there and felt inspired to volunteer. Tony had served in the Navy in the late 1960s, stationed on a ship equipped with guided missiles in the 6th Fleet. The park held special significance for him, as he recognized that it did for many other veterans. Both his father and father-in-law had served in World War II, deepening his connection to the place.

Tony and his wife, Olivia, soon began volunteering, greeting visitors, giving tours, and sharing stories about the park. They participated in special events, including the beautiful Christmas celebrations and tree lighting ceremonies. These events were particularly meaningful to veterans and their families, who would create or purchase special ornaments to honor loved ones who had served or fallen, placing them on the eighteen-foot Christmas tree that stood proudly in the park. Each year, the park was lit up in special ways for the holidays.

Chapter Seven

"Olivia and Tony Rubino-photo credit Ken Noon"

Their dedication did not go unnoticed, and they were invited to join the park's board. Tony and Olivia became part of the community of couples who contributed their time and passion to support the park. Olivia even purchased a commemorative granite tile featuring Tony, his father, and her father to celebrate their service.

"The folks there were so welcoming, and I consider Ken the real architect of the park," Tony said. "He has devoted so much time and energy over the years. I can't visit as often as I used to, but I still love it."

At the back of the park, there's a large open space where a Huey helicopter will eventually be displayed. In the meantime, an unexpected opportunity arose to acquire a military tank. Although not part of the park's original plan, the committee eagerly embraced the chance to display it in that vacant area.

The tank is an M60, a series that gained popularity during the Cold War, with production running from 1959 to 1962. Designed to replace the M48 Patton tank from World War II, the M60 featured a 105 mm main gun and composite armor, offering a balance of firepower and protection. It could reach speeds of up to 30 mph and had a range of 350 miles. Although the M60 has largely been retired from active service in the United States, it remains in use by some foreign militaries and has left a significant mark within the history of armored warfare.

This tank was crewed by four personnel, all stationed at the front, with the engine positioned at the back. It was also the last American tank design to include a floor-mounted escape hatch. This particular M60 saw service in Germany, where it was deployed to counter the growing presence of the Soviet T-54 tank, which had become widespread among the armies of the Warsaw Pact. Its final deployment was during Operation Desert Storm where it played a role before being retired.[3]

The M60 tank was generously offered to the park by VFW Post 3360 in Defiance, Ohio. On October 14, 2016, it was transported on a flatbed truck, making a slow journey of 180 miles to the trucking company lot on Route 224. The following morning, a special convoy was organized to cover the final sixty miles to the park, accompanied by a motorcycle escort. Mayor Al Knack, an enthusiastic motorcyclist, cut short his vacation in Florida to be part of the event. Though not a member of any veteran motorcycle groups, he was considered an honorary member and used his influence to rally support from various groups in Northeastern Ohio. Over the years, these groups had become deeply involved with the Ohio Veterans Memorial Park. On the day of the tank's arrival, the lead escorts were two prominent groups: Rolling Thunder, District 8, and the Ohio Patriot Guard Riders, District 3, joined by many other riders who wanted to participate.

Chapter Seven

"Flyer to gather all riders to accompany the tank-OVMP archives"

"It was freezing cold," Al recalled, "and we had every piece of weather gear we owned on our bodies for this ride. The man who owned the trucking yard sent his wife off in a pickup, and when she came back, the truck bed was full of donuts for us all. We ended up with hundreds of motorcycles escorting the tank that day."

As the convoy moved slowly along the highway, onlookers gathered on bridges, cheering and waving U.S. flags. "That was the coolest," Al reminisced, reflecting on the sense of unity and support from the community.

In preparation for the tank's arrival, Ken had set up four concrete pillars of varying heights with rubble and old broken tombstones around them, so when the crane positioned the tank, and ensuring the tank was securely set, it would give the illusion of moving over a low hill with a small tree crushed under its treads.

"The tank at night-OVMP archives"

Barbara Freeman later overheard a heartwarming message from the son of the owner of A&M Truck and Trailer Repair in Greenwich (the company responsible for transporting the tank). He had asked his father, "Dad, we aren't going to charge for moving this for the veterans' park, right?" and his father agreed without hesitation. Barbara, along with the park committee members, was deeply moved by this generous gesture, a testament to the support and goodwill the park continued to inspire.

Near the tank on the eastern side of the Vietnam Wall stands the Medal of Honor Memorial, dedicated in 2015. At the time, it was the only memorial of its kind, honoring recipients of the nation's highest military award. Established during the Civil War in 1861, the Medal of Honor symbolizes the utmost courage and selflessness in combat.

The Medal of Honor is unique in several respects. It is the highest military decoration awarded to U.S. service members, ranking above the Silver Star for valor and the Distinguished Service Cross. Recipients earn this honor for extraordinary acts of bravery during combat, often risking their lives to save others. The approval process is exceptionally rigorous, involving multiple investigations and recommendations from commanding officers, and the final authorization coming from the president of the United States.

One of the distinct honors associated with the Medal of Honor is that recipients are saluted by all military personnel, even those of higher rank. Additionally, they receive a lifetime stipend, invitations to prestigious events (including presidential inaugurations), and the right to be buried with full military honors at Arlington National Cemetery. The medal can also be awarded posthumously, recognizing acts of valor by those who have made the ultimate sacrifice.

On July 25, 1963, the criteria for the Medal of Honor were standardized across all branches of the U.S. military, specifying that recipients must have "distinguished themselves conspicuously by gallantry and intrepidity at the risk of their lives, above and beyond the call of duty."[4]

There are three versions of the Medal of Honor, each designated for different branches of the U.S. military: Army, Air Force, and Navy (which also covers the Marine Corps and Coast Guard). The Medal of Honor Memorial at the park features representations of each medal on three sides, each design reflecting the unique characteristics of its respective military branch.

During the Korean War, 146 service members were awarded the Medal of Honor, including four from Ohio. In the Vietnam War, the number of recipients rose to 240, thirteen from Ohio. Each of these medals honor acts of extraordinary bravery and sacrifice, preserving the legacy of those who served with unparalleled courage.

"Medal of Honor monument-OVMP archives"

Rodger Wilton Young[5] was a Sergeant in the Ohio National Guard, but he made the unusual request to be demoted to private just before his unit was called to serve in World War II. Despite being a skilled marksman, even with his thick Coke bottle glasses, and an effective infantry squad leader, Rodger was struggling with hearing loss. He felt this impairment could hinder his ability to lead his men in combat, so he chose to step down from his leadership role.

Growing up in Tiffin, Ohio, Rodger—nicknamed "Fuzz"—was a rural boy with a passion for sports. At just five feet, two inches tall, he didn't have the typical physique for athletics, but he played with determination and enthusiasm. During a high school basketball game, he suffered a severe head injury after being knocked down, leaving him unconscious for hours and requiring hospitalization. Although he recovered, the long-term effects were significant: He was left nearly blind and partially deaf, forcing him to leave school. In 1937, during peacetime, he and his brother joined the National Guard, seeking financial stability rather than out of a sense of patriotism.

By 1943, Rodger's unit, the 37th Infantry, was called to action in the Solomon Islands, where the Marines were engaged in fierce battles for control. Rodger's family often said his heart was bigger than his body, and that was evident in the decision he made. Aware of his worsening hearing, he approached his commanding officer to explain that he could no longer serve as a leader. "I don't want any of my men killed in New Georgia because of me," he said. Rodger wanted to take responsibility only for himself, knowing it was the best way to protect the men under his command.

Rodger Wilton Young's heroism is immortalized in his Medal of Honor citation, which reads:

> On 31 July 1943, the infantry company of which Pvt. Young was a member was ordered to make a limited withdrawal from the battle line to adjust the battalion's position for the night. At this time, Pvt. Young's platoon was engaged with the enemy in a dense jungle where observation was very limited. The platoon was suddenly pinned down by intense fire from a Japanese machine gun concealed on higher ground, only 75 yards away. The initial burst wounded Pvt. Young. As the platoon began to obey the order to withdraw, Pvt. Young

called out that he could see the enemy emplacement, and he began creeping toward it. Another burst from the machine gun wounded him a second time. Despite his injuries, he continued his heroic advance, drawing enemy fire and responding with his own rifle. When he was close enough to his target, he began throwing hand grenades, and while doing so, was hit again and killed. Pvt. Young's bold action in engaging the Japanese pillbox, thereby diverting its fire, allowed his platoon to withdraw without further losses and resulted in several enemy casualties.

For his extraordinary bravery, Pvt. Young was posthumously awarded the Medal of Honor. His legacy endures in many forms that continue to honor his sacrifice. There is a park named after him, an Ohio National Guard training site that bears his name, and even a fictional troop transport in a novel that pays tribute to him. In August 2021, a Medal of Honor marker was dedicated to him at the Ohio Veterans Memorial Park, sponsored by the National Society of the Daughters of the American Revolution, Akron Chapter.

Rodger Young's story also inspired a popular song titled "The Ballad of Rodger Young" by Frank Loesser, which became well known in 1945. The final stanza captures the essence of his legacy:

> Shines the name—Rodger Young,
> Fought and died for the men he marched among.
> To the everlasting glory of the Infantry
> Lives the story of Private Rodger Young.

Rodger Young's courage and selfless actions continue to be a source of pride for his family and an enduring symbol of bravery for the nation.

Chapter Seven

Most Americans are familiar with the Medal of Honor and the Purple Heart, but there are many other medals that recognize acts of valor. Each of these awards represents bravery, sacrifice, and the bloodshed of America's finest. Understanding military awards can be complex, as valor is recognized through a range of medals that have been created over time.

The Medal of Honor, established during the Civil War, was the nation's only valor award until 1918, when the Distinguished Service Cross was introduced during World War I. As countless acts of bravery occurred, a hierarchy of awards became necessary to distinguish levels of heroism. Alongside the Medal of Honor and Distinguished Service Cross, other medals were established, including the Silver Star, Distinguished Flying Cross, Bronze Star, Air Medal, and Commendation Medal.

The Bronze Star and the Commendation Medal can also be awarded with a "V" device to denote acts of heroism, further distinguishing acts of valor for meritorious service. While medals are a formal recognition of extraordinary courage, most soldiers display bravery and resilience every day, with or without an award to mark their sacrifices.

Beallsville, Ohio, a small town in Monroe County with a population of fewer than five hundred, experienced a heartbreaking loss during the Vietnam War. From 1966 to 1971, the community lost seven young men to the conflict. Despite desperate appeals from residents to lawmakers, urging them to stop drafting local boys after the deaths of the first five, their pleas were ignored. By the war's end, two more young men from this tiny town had made the ultimate sacrifice, underscoring the profound impact of the war on such a small community.

A similar story of loss unfolded in a town nearby Clinton—Wadsworth, Ohio, a town of around twenty thousand residents at the time. Thirteen young men from Wadsworth died during the Vietnam

War, but for decades their sacrifice went unrecognized with no official town memorial. Determined to honor their memory, family members joined forces to fundraise for a memorial bench to be placed at the Ohio Veterans Memorial Park. Their efforts resulted in the Wadsworth 13 bench, situated near the Gold Star Mother memorial and serving as a poignant reminder of the extraordinary loss suffered by this small town.

Cuyahoga Falls, another nearby community with a population of less than fifty thousand in the 1970s, faced a similar tragedy. Thirteen of its young men were killed in the Vietnam War, devastating the town as one death followed another. In response, residents came together to commission a memorial bench, funded by donations, with the names of their fallen sons engraved on it. This bench now sits near the Wadsworth 13 bench, symbolizing the collective grief and sacrifice shared by these communities.

Amid the excitement of acquisitions, dedications, and a flurry of activities, troubling behaviors surfaced within the organization. One of the common challenges faced by volunteer groups is the theft or misappropriation of funds. Without proper oversight and preventive measures, embezzlement and fraudulent reporting can occur, often due to misplaced trust or a lack of safeguards.

This issue affected the OVMP, impacting both the volunteer committee and the community it serves. Over an extended period, several thousand dollars were allegedly diverted for personal use by an individual entrusted with financial responsibilities. Initially, the misappropriation went unnoticed, and when it finally came to light, it was a shock to the entire group. The members had worked tirelessly for every dollar raised, and discovering unethical behavior from someone they trusted shook the integrity of the organization. Difficult decisions about how to address the situation followed. Beyond the immediate financial loss, there was the risk of undermining public trust, which could damage the organization's reputation and lead to reduced donations.

Some committee members had experienced the scandal in 2009–2010, and the fear of losing donor confidence, decreased volunteer engagement, and potential legal consequences—including lawsuits, penalties, or even dissolution—was all too real. The committee collaborated with the appropriate state agencies to resolve the issues and restore integrity.

Key lessons emerged from this experience. Members were reminded to never sign off on meeting minutes or budgets without thoroughly reviewing and agreeing with them. Regular financial audits became essential for maintaining transparency, along with clear operational policies. Additionally, having two people manage donations and budgets not only provided a system of checks and balances but also helped share the workload of volunteer labor, ensuring greater accountability.

"Daniel Patron-courtesy of the Patron family"

Sergeant Daniel J. Patron of Canton, Ohio, was known for his million-dollar smile and his dedication as an EOD (explosive ordinance disposal) technician. He served with the 8th Engineer Support Battalion, 2nd Marine Logistics Group, II Marine Expeditionary Force, based at Camp Lejeune, NC. On August 6, 2011, Daniel lost his life while conducting combat operations to defuse roadside bombs in Helmand Province, Afghanistan. Those who knew him say he embraced life with passion, driven by a desire to make his family proud by being the best Marine he could be. He was known for loving unconditionally and sacrificing without hesitation.

Chapter Seven

Daniel served two tours in Iraq and one in Afghanistan, earning a reputation as a remarkable warrior. His brother Matthew created a full-length documentary titled *Collecting Sgt. Dan*,[6] which is available on Prime Video. The film captures the heartfelt memories and struggles of Dan's comrades as they share stories of his life and his ultimate sacrifice. It concludes with a poignant segment showing the tattoos that friends and family have gotten in Dan's memory, reflecting their journey of healing and the enduring legacy of Sgt. Dan. Through this documentary, Matt aimed to preserve his brother's story, offering a sense of healing for the family and a tribute to Dan's life.

In school, Dan was a fun-loving presence, participating in choir, school plays, speech and debate, and in band as a drummer. His mother Kathy was his teacher and coach on the high school speech and debate team. He even wrote several drum riffs for his high school band. He had a deep love for his wife and family, rescue dogs and motorbikes. Those who knew him spoke of the positive impact he had on everyone he met. Over the years, numerous services and monuments have been dedicated to honoring Dan Patron's life and legacy.

At the Ohio Veterans Memorial Park, a simple black granite bench bears his picture, name, rank, and dates of service. On the day of its dedication, a couple hundred people gathered on the east side of the wall to pay their respects. Unbeknownst to the crowd, the Perry High School drum corps had set up on the west side of the wall, hidden from view. Arranged as a surprise, they played Dan's compositions during the ceremony, a gesture that deeply moved everyone present.

At a service honoring Dan Patron, a Marine colleague quoted G. K. Chesterton, an early twentieth-century British author, saying, "The true soldier fights not because he hates what is in front of him, but because he loves what is behind him." This sentiment perfectly encapsulates the spirit of Sgt. Dan Patron, who lived and served with love, dedication, and an unwavering sense of duty.

"Ohio Vietnam Wall in snow-OVMP archives"

CHAPTER EIGHT

Poems are moments' monuments.

—Sylvia Plath

2017–2020

If you were head over heels in love and attended Mansfield High School in Ohio during the mid-1960s, you might have sought out Kay Trumpower, the poet in residence, during school hours anyway. For fifty cents, she would write a personalized love poem for your sweetheart, using the money she earned to buy lunch. The oldest of fifteen children, Kay's entrepreneurial spirit emerged early.

"I didn't want to brown-bag it in high school for lunch, and things were tight at home," she explained. Kay began writing poetry almost as soon as she could write, devouring every book of poetry she could find. She also had a natural talent for crafts, art, and arranging flowers, and she used these skills to supplement her income. She had a love for beautiful things and found ways to share that love creatively.

Kay went on to cofound the Kingwood Herb Society, and she spent over a decade teaching K–12 students about the history of herbs and food. Her motivation was not just financial but also stemmed from a passion for her interests. Yet through it all, poetry remained a constant in her life.

After her husband, Tom McNaul, a Vietnam veteran, passed away from liver cancer related to Agent Orange, Kay's health declined, and she found herself battling depression and loneliness. But poetry became her lifeline, eventually leading to a connection with Derek Kleinknecht. Derek began taking photographs to accompany her poems, and one day he surprised her with a trip to the Ohio Veterans Memorial Park.

There, poetry once again became a bridge—this time to Ken Noon, who happened to be at the park that day. After discussing her passion, Ken asked if she would write a special poem for the Vietnam wall, honoring the 3,095 souls it represented. Kay obliged. It is named "The 3095" and was engraved at the north end of the wall. She proudly read it to the crowd during the Veterans Day commemoration on November 11, 2011. "It was thrilling," she recalled.

A couple of years later, Ken requested another poem, this time for the new *Gold Star Father* statue at the park. Kay wrote it, and it is carved into the base of the statue. She attempted to read it at the dedication ceremony. "I followed the Gold Star Fathers who spoke, and I could barely get the poem out. I did, but I broke down," she admitted.

With Derek's photography and Kay's gifts for poetry and art, they collaborated to create striking pieces of military art that now adorn the walls of the David F. Winder Mansfield VA Clinic, a newer, larger facility where their work makes a powerful statement. They continue to work together on various projects, selling their creations throughout the region, but military art remains their specialty.

"I don't think anyone else is doing what we do to honor our veterans, and what an honor it has been to write poems," Kay A. McNaul said modestly. "I am blessed. The pen is moving God's ink."

Chapter Eight

"Kay McNaul with one of her many poems displayed at the David F. Winder Veteran Mansfield VA Clinic, Mansfield, Ohio-OVMP archives"

Sometimes, a soldier is also a writer and a poet. Such was the case with Vincent Lavery, a valiant Vietnam veteran. His wife Ruth and daughter Danielle, both served on the board of the Ohio Veterans Memorial Park, and Danielle remains the park board's treasurer. Vincent, who served as a field medic in Vietnam from July 1968 to the Christmas holidays of 1969, had a passion for writing and often reflected on his time in the Army.

Known by his family as a warm, funny, and supportive man, Vincent was devoted to his wife, two daughters, and extended family, especially the children. He shared a particularly close bond with his niece Christi, Danielle's cousin, who was especially fond of her uncle Vince.

Despite falling ill from war-related causes, he continued to read and write extensively, particularly about his wartime experiences and the bonds he shared with his fellow soldiers. In *The Almanac of Vietnam War*,[1] he'd underlined certain battles they were in by exclaiming next to it: "I was there!" He earned two Bronze Stars and a Purple Heart.

"Vincent Lavery-courtesy of the Lavery family"

Vincent came from a military family. His father, James, served in the Navy aboard the USS *Finback* during World War II and was among the crew who rescued President George H. W. Bush after he was shot down as a pilot. When Bush became president, Vincent sought to reconnect his father with him. When President Bush visited Akron, his staff arranged a meeting at Tangier's restaurant, where they could reminisce about the wartime rescue.

Chapter Eight

"Vincent Lavery in Vietnam-courtesy of the Lavery family"

In a Memorial Day edition of the *Akron Beacon Journal*, he published a deeply emotional and heartfelt piece about the camaraderie he found during the war:

> Summer is near and the first "Party" of the season is here. All through the towns and villages, banners stretch across streets proclaiming the celebration at hand. Family and friends will gather in backyards—burgers on the grill, iron shoes cutting through the air to their marks. Boaters will take to the lakes with their sun-drenched crew. And the booze will flow all weekend long.
>
> America loves a party.

As for myself, I think I'll go for a walk. Clear the years from my cluttered mind and drift back to a time that waits for me. To a place where a group of young boys were cast together so many miles from home. I'll think of the time we spent together. The good and the bad, and how we became men, and cried, and how we became warriors, and died.

I'll remember huddling together in the mud of the monsoon, and how we played a trick on Mommason for cigarettes. I'll recall the time we celebrated with Poppason the New Year—snake cakes and rice wine from a Jim Beam bottle. I'll remember burning his village to the ground. I'll walk and recall my buddies who made it or those who didn't.

I'll laugh when I think of Mike and how he managed to stay out of combat shamming on a superficial leg wound. Or Cliff, who led a wake down a mine-strewn road, and how the villagers honored him. I'll wipe my eyes and cough a little and see Jack and Jim and Pineapple, the Hawaiian.

And I'll remember John, who in an act of heroism stopped a sliver of steel with his heart. As he lay there in my arms, he looked up and asked, "Am I going home, Doc?" and as I wiped the sweat of the jungle from his face and whispered, "Yeah, John, you're going home."

I'll stop where I'm at, raise my arm to the sky, spread my fingers in salute, and say, "Here's to you fellas. The party's still going; only thing is you weren't invited."

Chapter Eight

I love you.

I miss you.

Vincent P. Lavery, Marshallville

Vincent passed away in 2016, leaving behind a family who loved him and his words that captured the spirit of brotherhood and resilience formed on the battlefield.

Sometimes, a single person's deep commitment and enthusiasm for a project can leave a lasting impact. At the Ohio Veterans Memorial Park, that person is Sergeant Johnnie Downs, affectionately known to all as Sgt. Downs. Beyond his personal dedication to honoring his brother Herman and his family's military legacy—beautifully commemorated on a memorial bench at the park—Sgt. Downs has shown unwavering patriotic devotion to the OVMP community over the years.

"Granite tiles dedicated to brothers, Herman and Johnnie Downs-OVMP archives"

A true champion of the contributions of African American and Native American regiments in U.S. war efforts, Sgt. Downs has worked tirelessly to ensure their enduring legacies are recognized. He spearheaded fundraising efforts and collaborated with Summit Memorials to create six monuments along the park's History Walk, a brick pathway that extends from the center of the eastern side of the wall to the Medal of Honor monument. Through his efforts, these monuments serve as a powerful tribute to the diverse and heroic contributions of these communities throughout U.S. military history.

The monuments along the park's History Walk are commissioned by individuals who believe there are significant figures and events in U.S. military history that deserve recognition. Among those who have taken on this mission is Sgt. Johnnie Downs, who has been instrumental in ensuring that these stories are told.

Sgt. Downs commissioned monuments honoring

- **Dan Bullock**, the youngest Marine to die in Vietnam;
- the **Tuskegee Airmen**, the first African American aviators who served in WWII;
- **Rocky Bleier**, an NFL player who was drafted, wounded in combat, and returned to the NFL to win four Super Bowls;
- the **African American Ranger Airborne Company** of the Korean War;
- **Pat Tillman**, who left his NFL career, donated his military pay, became an Army Ranger, and was killed in action in Afghanistan in 2004;
- the **Infantry Combat Badge**, recognizing the consistent, tough missions carried out by infantrymen and the unique dangers they face.

CHAPTER EIGHT

"Monument dedicated to the black rangers-OVMP archives"

Sgt. Downs is now working on a new monument to honor the Navajo Code Talkers, who used their language as a secret means of communication in World War II. Their unbreakable code was credited with contributing to decisive victories throughout the war.

Sgt. Downs's selflessness and dedication to preserving history make him a role model for future generations. His commitment to honoring these legacies shows a deep sense of identity and history and a belief in something greater than himself—qualities that are undoubtedly heroic.

In addition to the monuments Sgt. Downs has sponsored, there are other memorials along the History Walk, including

- the **U.S. Navy Armed Guard**, a branch of the Navy disbanded after WWII;
- the **U.S. Merchant Marines**, recognizing civilian volunteers who served during WWII;

- a monument dedicated to the **Vietnam War dead from Lorain County, Ohio**.

These memorials, collectively, tell a broader story of courage, sacrifice, and the diverse contributions of those who served.

Gary watched the trucks rumbling past, kicking up dust. Dark thoughts crept in—he considered throwing himself under the massive wheels or using a grenade to end it all. All over a letter.

In 1966, Gary was drafted to then join the 101st Army Airborne deploying in 1967 to Vietnam, leaving behind his girlfriend of two years, Barbara, in Manchester, Ohio. Fresh out of high school, he entered the chaos of war with one thing keeping him grounded: his love for Barbara. But one day, he received a letter that shattered him more than any mortar blast could.

Throughout history, news from home has been a cherished escape for soldiers in the midst of war. Many have said that aside from news of going home, mail was the most important thing to them. Every day, thirteen thousand pounds of mail would arrive in Da Nang, Vietnam, to be distributed to the various regions where soldiers' hearts would leap at the sound of "MAIL CALL!" Letters from home, boxes of treats, hometown newspapers, magazines, catalogs, and, too often, the dreaded Dear John letters.[2]

For Gary, Tuesday was mail day. He was out in the field when his letter arrived. Barb had written to say she had been convinced by friends to "date around" and no longer considered Gary her exclusive boyfriend. It was a direct hit to his heart and ego. Someone else would try to take his place with the woman he loved.

He had been carrying a ring with him—one he bought for Barbara. It was a symbol of his love, and he took it everywhere in Vietnam, a reminder of the warmth and affection that kept him going in such a hostile environment. Now, that connection was broken, leaving him adrift.

Soldiers are often superstitious, carrying good luck charms or tokens to help them feel a sense of control amid the chaos. For Gary, Barbara's loving words had been his anchor, and the ring was his talisman. If those words and that symbol had kept him safe, what would their absence mean for his chances of survival?

Only weeks later, another letter arrived—another Dear John from Barb. He wondered, hadn't she hurt him enough the first time?

Love can be difficult under any circumstance, but during the hardships of war, a breakup can devastate a young man who depends on that long-distance relationship to sustain his morale. Known as "Dear John" letters since World War II, these were essentially breakup letters sent to soldiers from their girlfriends or wives back home, often informing them that the relationship has ended. Sometimes, it was because the woman had found someone else in the soldier's absence. Regardless of the reason, the emotional toll on the young men receiving these letters was profound. It could leave them despondent, reckless in battle, and without the motivation to make it back home.

Gary was injured on Mother's Day in 1968 when his military truck hit a roadside bomb, leading to his hospitalization. That day, his mother had a premonition that something had happened to him. Soon after, Gary was headed home. When his mother asked if she should invite Barb to the airport for his homecoming, he agreed—though he didn't hold out much hope that she would show up. During his time in the hospital, his belongings were ransacked; among the stolen items were his numerous medals and the ring he had carried for Barb, leaving him feeling particularly low.

As he stepped off the plane, his family was there to greet him. And then, in the shadows near the doorway, he saw Barb, "looking gorgeous. She was all I could see," Gary recalled. She admitted to him that she had briefly dated two other boys while he was away, but reassured him that "nothing happened." Despite the uncertainty that lingered from her letters, they married the following year and have now been together for fifty-five years.

Gary still wonders about those two Dear John letters. "Was I supposed to answer the first one?" he mused, as neither of them was entirely clear on Dear John letter etiquette. Barb had expected a reply. "I simply couldn't be sure that he got the first one," she explained. In the end, their love endured, overcoming the misunderstandings and the miles between them.

Families often grew anxious when they didn't hear from their young soldiers, but sometimes it was simply because their loved ones weren't the best at keeping in touch. PFC Tom Whims was one of those noncommunicative soldiers, especially during the early days of his service. From a young age, Tom had always known he would become a soldier following a family tradition of military service. His mother would often encourage him, saying, "Eat those vegetables so you can grow into a strong soldier someday!"

Even as an adult, his mother still looked out for him. When Tom failed to send letters home from boot camp, she grew concerned. Undeterred, she reached out through her connections until word of her worry made its way to Tom's commanding officer. Tom eventually sent a letter home, but it came with a clear message: "Don't ever contact my CO again like that!" And as a playful nod to their old mealtime conversations, he added, "P.S., I'm still not eating my vegetables!"

Chapter Eight

Tom went on to rise through the ranks, becoming a Sergeant and making his mother very proud. Despite the rocky start to his correspondence, his humor and dedication shone through, reminding his family that he was doing just fine.

"Thomas Whims-courtesy of the Whims family"

Among the park's benches stands a statue of a black Labrador retriever. Around its neck is a collar bearing the name "Dagger." At first glance, it may seem like an unusual addition to a veterans' memorial park, but a closer look at the inscriptions on the nearby memorial bench reveals its significance.

The bench is dedicated to the "Combat Tracker Teams of Vietnam" and features the silhouette of five men and a dog. The men are armed, except for the dog handler, and none are wearing combat helmets. The inscription reads, "In memory of the men and dogs who gave their all," along with the names of over forty men and thirteen canines. These teams were highly specialized and operated with a level of secrecy, both during their missions in Vietnam and for many years after.

Few Americans are familiar with the story of the Combat Tracker Teams (CTT), elite units of men and dogs who were committed to "out-guerrilla the guerrillas" in the dense jungles of Southeast Asia during the Vietnam War. Operating with exceptional skill and training, the CTT was a secretive program that ran from 1967 until 1971 when it was discontinued. Tracking was essential in the jungle terrain and oppressive heat of Vietnam, where the enemy would frequently vanish after ambushes, making it difficult for U.S. forces to maintain contact. This method of tracking had never been utilized in U.S. warfare before.

John and Donna Carroll were longtime volunteers and committee members at the Ohio Veterans Memorial Park (OVMP). John, an Army sergeant and Vietnam veteran, served as a visual tracker on CTT #4, which was attached to the 4th Infantry Division in Pleiku in 1968, covering the Central Highlands. He also became an instructor at the British Army Jungle Warfare Training School, where CTT training was conducted. The concept of combat tracking had been developed by the British to combat Communist insurgents in Malaysia during the 1950s.

The New Zealand Special Air Service joined the British in refining the training at the school in Malaysia, and both nations, along with the U.S., supplied the dogs—primarily Labrador retrievers—chosen for their keen noses and calm dispositions. Each CTT consisted of five men: a visual tracker, a dog handler, a cover man, a radio operator, a team leader, and, of course, the dog. The men had to be incredibly fit, with heightened senses and specialized training. Their preparation included airborne training, intelligence gathering, and high-security clearance. The jungle became their second home, and the teamwork between the men had to be flawless, as their lives—and the lives of other soldiers—depended on it.

CTTs operated without helmets or flak jackets, as these were too cumbersome for their fast, silent movements. Their mission was not to lead troops but to perform several critical tasks:

1. Re-establish contact with the enemy after an attack and when the opposition has disappeared into the jungle.

2. Locate enemy mortar and rocket installations.

3. Track enemy snipers and land-mine layers.

4. Track hostile parties spotted by ground or air.

5. Find lost or missing friendly patrols or personnel.

6. Gather vital intelligence on enemy movements and positions.

Each of these missions could mean the difference between life and death for soldiers. And often, the CTTs had stories of their dogs saving their lives. The Labradors excelled at their tracking duties, alerting the men to nearby enemies or hidden booby traps. They provided not only essential service but also companionship and unconditional love, which the men returned wholeheartedly.[3]

An informative book on this subject is *Seek On! Combat Trackers in Vietnam* by Susan Merritt,[4] which explores the experiences of these teams in depth. The CTT dogs were more than just tools of war, they were loyal companions, often affectionately called "good boys" or "good girls" by the soldiers they protected. Their work saved countless lives, and the bond between the dogs and their handlers and teams was built on mutual trust and affection, making their contributions and sacrifices an enduring part of the untold history of the Vietnam War.

For decades, the Combat Tracker Teams received no recognition for their quiet and critical operations. The nature of their work kept them out of the spotlight, and those involved rarely spoke about it. It wasn't until 2,000, decades after their service, that these teammates reunited for one of the first CTT reunions, marking a long-overdue acknowledgment of their contributions.

Donna Carroll discovered information about a reunion online and mentioned it to John. Having never discussed Vietnam with anyone since returning home, John was initially hesitant. "No," he said, uncertain if he was ready to revisit that part of his life. But with time, he changed his mind and has since embraced reconnecting with his fellow CTT members. Now he is proud of his service, and he believes it's time for the rest of the country to fully recognize the bravery and sacrifices of these men. Many soldiers returned home alive because of the work and dedication of the CTT.

In June 2013, John hosted a CTT reunion at the OVMP in Clinton. "It was really wonderful!" Donna recalled. During the event, the granite memorial bench and the black Lab statue were dedicated, paying tribute to the fallen CTT members—both human and canine. The dedication served as a long-awaited moment of healing and a proper farewell to those who gave their lives.

Chapter Eight

"Statue of Dagger and the bench celebrating the Combat Tracker Teams-photo credit Cliff Franks"

The statue's dog, Dagger, was named after the lab who served on John's CTT in Vietnam. Unfortunately, the soldiers were not allowed to bring their dogs home due to concerns about disease, a heartbreaking reality for those who had formed deep bonds with their canine companions. In honor of his old partner, John named his black Lab at home "Dagger." That beloved dog passed away last year at the age of thirteen. Today, a new black Lab pup, named Sabre, lives with the Carroll's. "He is full of energy. He's a good boy," John said warmly. "A good boy."

At the park, many benches are placed by communities and organizations to honor veterans. Some are dedicated to living veterans by friends, families, or groups, while others commemorate one or more soldiers who made the ultimate sacrifice. These tributes ensure that the legacies of service, bravery, and sacrifice endure for generations to come.

In 2017, a group of young, patriotic Americans made a heartfelt contribution to the Ohio Veterans Memorial Park by donating a memorial bench. The children and educators of Orrville Elementary School, led by Principal Beverly Waseman, has been honoring veterans for many years. "I believe it is of vital importance to get school-age children involved with our military veterans," said Beverly. Each year, she organized Veterans Day parades through the school's hallways where local veterans in uniform would march while the children applauded, celebrating and honoring their service.

Orrville, a town of about 8,500 in Wayne County, is home to one of America's largest jelly companies, The J.M. Smucker Company. It attracts summer tourists with its picturesque rural Amish country scenes, complete with horse-drawn buggies, farmland, and charming shops and restaurants.

Every November, Orrville Elementary raises money through a penny war competition, where each grade tries to collect more donated pennies than the others. One year, Beverly suggested to the Parent-Teacher Organization that they use the funds to purchase a memorial bench for the park. She believed it would be a lasting way to honor veterans and show the children the importance of celebrating and respecting those who served. The idea was eagerly accepted, and soon the children were involved in designing and ordering the bench, excited to see their contributions take shape.

Chapter Eight

"Day out at the OVMP. Orville school children here to help and dedicate their bench-courtesy of Beverly Waseman"

Ken invited Beverly to bring the kids for a field trip for when the bench was being installed. While she loved the idea, there were seven hundred children in the school, making a full trip impractical. Instead, they decided that representatives from the fourth-grade student council and the third-grade character council would attend on that special day, emphasizing the school district's commitment to character development.

Beverly recalled the experience as one that she was sure the students would remember for a lifetime. "We had the best time," she exclaimed. The day was filled with activities, including a guided tour, an informative talk, and a scavenger hunt. The children watched as the bench was carefully placed with a crane, and they enjoyed their packed lunches in the Family of Heroes Hall before heading back to school, full of stories to share. Later, Sharon Kerechanin, who had helped organize the day, sent dog tags and OVMP picture postcards for the school's bulletin boards, further commemorating the experience.

One of the Vietnam veterans who participated in the annual school parades once approached Beverly during the Veterans Day festivities. He confided, "People threw rocks at me when I got home from Vietnam. These children really do my heart good." His words reinforced Beverly's belief that their efforts to honor veterans were making a genuine difference. For her, it was a reminder that teaching children to appreciate and respect those who serve is a lesson that resonates far beyond the classroom.

"The hard-earned bench from the school children of Orville- courtesy of Beverly Waseman"

Chapter Eight

Another poignant memorial at the OVMP is the Fallen Soldier Cross, also known as the Battlefield Cross,[5] a symbol that has its roots in the American Civil War. Originally, a fallen soldier's rifle was thrust bayonet-first into the ground, leaving the butt end pointed skyward, serving as a marker to identify the soldier's quick burial. Additional personal items were often placed nearby to signify the individual.

Today, the Battlefield Cross remains a powerful symbol, especially since soldiers in modern conflicts are rarely able to attend the funerals of their fallen comrades. The elements of the cross convey deep meaning:

- The rifle is thrust into the ground, representing a soldier who fought to the end.
- The boots, worn and dirty, are placed at the base of the rifle, symbolizing the final journey taken to battle for freedom.
- Dog tags hang from the rifle, signifying the identity of the fallen, ensuring they are never forgotten.
- The helmet is placed atop the rifle, denoting that the soldier stood for liberty and fought bravely but their battle has come to an end.

"The battlefield cross above the POW pond-OVMP archives"

At the OVMP, the Battlefield Cross is positioned above the waterfall in a serene sitting area. Enclosed in a plexiglass box, this memorial represents all wars, incorporating a mix of belongings from different eras. It is a deeply moving image, embodying the tremendous sacrifice of U.S. soldiers who have given their lives in service to their country.

"If we can't smoke cigars, drink a beer, and ride motorcycles, let me go," Robert L. Gilbert II told his father six months before he was fatally shot by a single bullet from a high-powered rifle on March 8, 2010. They had been discussing life support, a conversation not unfamiliar to soldiers and their families. Robert made it clear he did not want to be kept alive by machines if it meant sacrificing the life he cherished.

Robert had been a Marine for nearly ten years, enlisting at eighteen. By the age of twenty-seven, he had risen to the rank of gunnery sergeant, one of the youngest to achieve that rank in the U.S. Marine Corps. As a gunnery sergeant, he held significant responsibility as an operations

Chapter Eight

chief and tactical advisor overseeing training and planning at command posts and operation centers.

On his five tours of duty, Robert was deployed from Iraq to Afghanistan, his most recent tour supporting combat operations in Badghis Province. He was assigned to the 2nd Military Special Operations Battalion, Marine Special Operations Regiment, Marine Corps Forces Special Operation Command, based at Camp Lejeune, NC. Two weeks before his death, Robert had been shot, but a bulletproof vest saved his life. He later confided to others that he felt like a target for the Taliban, sharing his concerns with his girlfriend but asking her to keep them from his father.

"Gunnery Sergeant Robert L. Gilbert II-courtesy of the Gilbert family"

On March 8, a bullet pierced his helmet, and he was medevacked to Germany before being transferred stateside to the National Naval Medical Center in Bethesda, MD, where he remained in a coma. His father, Bob Gilbert, a police officer and medic-fire specialist, was able to accompany him throughout the journey. Robert never regained consciousness, and Bob was faced with the painful decision to honor his son's wishes, ultimately removing life support. In his final act as a father, Bob chose to protect his son from unnecessary pain, knowing that this was what Robert wanted, despite the heartache it caused.

On March 16, 2010, Robert's twenty-eighth birthday, family, friends, and hospital staff gathered to sing "Happy Birthday" as the clock passed midnight. Bob held his son's hand, reflecting on when he'd been the medic assisting his wife when Robert was born in 1982. He laid his hand on his son's chest as Robert took his last breath, whispering, "I love you. Thank you for being my son. I enjoyed the twenty-eight years to the month and day we have shared together."

Every year, the local Amvets Post 176 organizes a memorial poker run in Robert's honor, led by Bob. Between two and three hundred bikers participate, riding about 110 miles to celebrate Robert's life and sacrifice. Funds raised during the event support Fisher House's Hero Miles Program in Robert's name, helping families of service members travel to be with their loved ones during medical treatment. Family and friends continue to gather each year on his birthday to honor his memory.

Gunnery Sergeant Robert Gilbert II has a section of Interstate 77 named after him and a memorial bench holds a place of honor near the brick walkway leading to the Marine flag. It bears a powerful inscription: "Some spend their entire lives wondering if they've made a difference in this world. The Marines don't have this problem." This tribute serves as a reminder of Robert's dedication, courage, and the lasting impact he made.

Chapter Eight

"Gilbert bench at night-photo credit Dan Draiss"

CHAPTER NINE

any man's death diminishes me,
because I am involved in Mankinde;
Therefore never send to know
For whom the bell tolls;
It tolls for thee.

—JOHN DONNE, *"For Whom the Bell Tolls"*

2021–2025

The Korean War (1950–1953), often called "The Forgotten War," earned its nickname because it was largely overshadowed by the end of World War II. It was never officially declared a war by Congress nor was it celebrated as a clear victory. Instead, the Korean War is often regarded as the first significant conflict of the Cold War era, marking the beginning of hostilities between the Democratic West and the Communist East.[1]

On July 23, 2022, the names of 1,822 Ohio Korean War heroes who lost their lives were dedicated on the east side of the Ohio Vietnam Wall. This is known by the veterans as the other front of the wall. The journey to inscribe these names is quite a story.

Bob McCullough is both a Vietnam War veteran and Korean War veteran; he was stationed in both Korea and Vietnam during his deployment from 1969 through 1971. He is a member of the park board and shares this account:

> The idea to honor Ohio's Korean War KIAs on the fifteen blank black granite panels emerged after a ceremony by the Korean War Veterans Association, Chapter 138, which dedicated a memorial bench on July 27, 2020. Bob Jones, a member of the group, initiated the effort. The *Akron Beacon Journal* attended and covered the event, highlighting the blank panels awaiting funding to commemorate these honorable soldiers. My contact information was included at the end of the article for those interested in contributing. Sadly, within the months following the bench dedication, many Korean veterans present that day passed away, never getting to see their comrades' names on the wall. This weighed heavily on my mind, especially as time was running out for these aging veterans.
>
> One survivor, John Stilles, had been shot twenty-two times by a North Korean zip gun, a crude, dangerous firearm. John only survived because the sub-zero temperatures in Korea that day slowed his bleeding. He passed away in 2020 at the age of eighty-seven, and his death motivated me to push harder to see those names engraved. By then, most of our chapter's members were between eighty-seven and ninety-five years old.
>
> A woman named Dolly Raines, whose husband Donald served in Korea, saw the article and donated life insurance funds in his honor, giving us the strong start we needed toward the over-$60,000 goal.

Chapter Nine

"Ken working on the Korean War names on the granite wall-photo credit Steve Wallis"

After meeting with Ken at Summit Memorials, we began the meticulous work of gathering names, comparing lists from various government sources. When the list was finalized, I started fundraising. I estimated it would take four years to reach the goal. I shared the costs with the seventeen Korean War chapters across Ohio, informing each chapter of the names associated with their areas. Soon, donations began to arrive. It took a little over a year to reach the goal.

Frank Thomas, a Korean War veteran from the chapter that placed the bench, asked his children to contribute to the project as a Christmas gift. They did, along with about 110 other donors who made the engraving possible. I had a banner created to display all the donors' names to honor them on the day the dedication took place.

The dedication of these names was a significant day of remembrance and celebration. The event featured a piano performance by Eun Young Lee, a Korean American musician with a doctor of music degree from the University of Michigan. Lee, who has won numerous competitions and performed at Carnegie Hall, captivated the audience. Throughout the day, the twenty-three-piece Moonlight Serenaders jazz big band played period music from the 1950s, accompanied by vocalists who looked like they had stepped straight out of that era.

White netting covered the wall and the engraved names. With dark clouds approaching and rain in the forecast, we started the event fifteen minutes early, hoping to get through it before the rain arrived. Despite our efforts, we got soaked as we unveiled the wall and dedicated the names. Yet, the spirits of the Korean veterans remained high, and we thought the rain was our brothers in heaven looking down moved to tears, showing us their appreciation for the 1822 names dedicated on the Korean Wall Memorial.

CHAPTER NINE

"General Robert D. Haas of Massillon, Ohio at the dedication of the Korean War names. He commanded an infantry platoon on the Main Line of Resistance in Korea in 1951-52-photo credit Steve Wallis"

The event's announcer was Don Stark, publisher of the military newspaper *DD214 Chronicle*, a newspaper for veterans. The colors were presented by uniformed Coast Guard members and Boy Scouts, followed by the unveiling of the names. A few dozen Korean War veterans, standing at attention if they were able, saluted as the music of their respective service branches played. "Taps" was sounded at the close of the event by Dave Harrison, a dedicated member of Bugles Across America who actively participates in many volunteer efforts across the area.

Despite facing numerous health issues over the past two decades, Dave has been a reliable presence, playing "Taps," "The Star-Spangled Banner," and other melodies on the trumpet and bugle at various events. Since 2010, he has become a fixture at dedications and memorial services, including holiday observances at the park.

"David Harrison playing Taps at the dedication of the names of Ohioans who died in the Korean War-photo credit Steve Wallis"

" 'Taps' consists of twenty-four notes and is instantly recognizable," Dave explained. "On Memorial Day, I visit the Ohio Western Reserve National Cemetery, moving through different areas of the park, and play 'Taps' twenty-four times, once for each note."

Chapter Nine

Dave is passionate about educating people on the nation's traditions, including the history and meaning behind "Taps." Though it is an instrumental piece, there are unofficial lyrics that capture the song's poignant message.

The first stanza reads:

Day is done.
Gone the sun.
From the lake,
From the hills,
From the sky.
All is well.
Safely rest.
God is nigh.

During one event, a woman asked Dave, "Do you charge for this?" Dave laughed and replied, "No. But I can play 'Charge.'" His humor and dedication have endeared him to many, making him a cherished part of the community's commemorative events.

Most events at the park, both large and small, are organized by the park board, which meets monthly or more frequently if needed. In the early days, fundraising efforts for the wall were so intensive that events often overlapped, reflecting the urgency of gathering support.

Chapters in the area of the National Society Daughters of the American Revolution (DAR) are active participants at the park, hosting several events throughout the year, including a free lunch for veterans each November. The Akron Chapter has also contributed by maintaining a beautiful perennial garden near the POW/MIA Reflecting Pond. These groups have been generous donors, supporting the park's upkeep and events.

While the Revolutionary War is not officially represented in the park's memorials—since Ohio became a state in 1803—the War of 1812 is the first conflict mentioned on the wall. Nevertheless, the DAR has established many monuments and benches throughout the park, honoring the legacy of those who have served and supporting the park's mission to remember all who fought for freedom.

Among the many fundraising activities organized by the Ohio Veterans Memorial Park, one stands out vividly in the memories of those who took part. The idea began in the summer of 2011, with Veterans Day (11/11/11) approaching. The previous year had been difficult, and no motorcycle run was held by the park committee, but veterans' motorcycle groups were always eager for a meaningful ride, and this event promised to be special.

The plan was ambitious: to create 3,095 flags, each bearing the name of a fallen Ohioan soldier from the Vietnam War listed on the wall. Each biker would then display a flag on their bike during the ride, with the goal of gathering as close to 3,095 motorcycles as possible. Since Veterans Day fell on a Friday that year, the ride was scheduled for the next day, Saturday, starting from a large staging area in Richfield, Ohio. Days Inn & Suites, with its expansive parking lots, agreed to host the event, which would see bikers travel from Richfield to the OVMP in Clinton. For those who didn't ride motorcycles, a sponsorship option was available that allowed them to purchase a hero's flag for a biker to carry.

The event required extensive coordination in the months leading up to it, and on the day of the ride, over two thousand motorcycles gathered. But the excitement was dampened by a tragic accident. Sean T. Simmons, a U.S. Navy veteran motorcyclist from Cuyahoga Falls, Ohio, was en route to join the 3,095 Ride when he lost control, veered

Chapter Nine

off the road, and hit a tree, dying instantly. His sudden passing was a shock to everyone, and the participants paused for prayers before the ride began, determined to honor the fallen.

That morning, the bikers assembled in Richfield, each carrying a black flag adorned with a heart colored purple and the name of a fallen veteran for the thirty-mile journey. Many riders took on the responsibility of carrying more than one flag. Arriving at the park marked the end of the journey for the bikers, but not for the flags.

"A flag representing a fallen Vietnam veteran that had been mounted on a motorcycle in the 11-11-2011 for the 3095 Ride-OVMP archives"

The ultimate goal was for the flags to find their way to the families of the fallen soldiers they represented. Where possible, the flags were taken home by the families at the park. Others were sent by mail, ensuring they reached their intended recipients. Friends also took flags to deliver to families or to keep and honor if no family members were left to claim them.

The 3,095 Ride became a powerful symbol of remembrance, community, and respect, connecting Ohioans to the sacrifices of their heroes and ensuring that the memory of each fallen soldier was carried, quite literally, on a journey of honor.

Around twelve hundred flags that had not been claimed by families during the 3,095 Ride were gathered at the park and eventually found their purpose in a very special project. These flags were sent to tech-savvy eighth graders in a history class at the National Inventors Hall of Fame School STEM (science, technology, engineering, and mathematics) Middle School in Akron, Ohio. The students had previously visited the Vietnam Memorial wall in Washington, D.C., and their teacher saw an opportunity for them to engage in a meaningful project with the OVMP.

During the semester they studied the Vietnam War, the students utilized their computer skills to locate contact information for the families of the names on the twelve hundred unclaimed flags. Through this project, they did more than just learn about history—they provided a valuable service, writing heartfelt letters to the families they were able to find.[2]

The students concluded their year with a field trip to the OVMP in Clinton where they could see the impact of their efforts firsthand. The park regularly welcomes students of all ages, with groups of elementary students often visiting in the late spring as part of their own field trips. This engagement with younger generations is central to the OVMP's mission:

> To interpret and preserve Ohio's military history for all generations for they may truly understand the cost of freedom. The park is to be a source of pride and solace to the families and comrades of the veterans honored there and to provide an unforgettable lesson in history to all who visit.

CHAPTER NINE

"Ariel drone picture of the Ohio Veterans Memorial Park, 2024-photo credit Jared McDaniel"

The veteran volunteers at the OVMP often credit their long-suffering wives and families, especially during the early years when so many hours were devoted to keeping the building project on track. Their support came with personal and professional sacrifices, as these families had to adjust to the demands placed on their time and energy.

The wives, in particular, were the unsung heroes behind the park's success. Their influence was felt at events where they worked quietly behind the scenes, helping to feed volunteers and ensure everything ran smoothly. At home, they maintained stability, managing family life while their husbands dedicated extra hours each week to the park.

There were inevitable strains and stresses, and many family events were missed. Yet, despite the challenges, most will tell you that the sacrifices were worth it, knowing they contributed to something lasting and meaningful. Barb Kindig is proud of Gary's accomplishment as president of the park the past few years, "He's done a great job! We don't let it overtake our lives though."

Several couples have shared their commitment to the OVMP, often serving as board members together and working side by side on various projects. They supported the park during military holiday vigils, fed the crowds, parked the cars, and played key roles in fundraising events like golf outings and car shows. Their efforts extended to hands-on tasks, including digging the pond and unloading the helicopter.

Looking back, many recall those years as a time of accomplishment and camaraderie, marked by great friendships and a strong sense of purpose. Though time has passed and their responsibilities have shifted, which has led them to step back from their volunteer roles, they carry fond memories of their time at the park. The experience reinforced a sense of togetherness within the veteran community, a bond that remains strong even after their active involvement has ended.

An important community link for the park is Judge Edward J. Elum who has served the Massillon Municipal Court District for twenty-nine years. In November 2019, he was re-elected to his fifth term in office. The judge established a veterans' assistance and treatment program in collaboration with the Stark County Veterans Service Commission, which included an assigned service officer. Additionally, he and Judge Joel C. Fichter developed a successful license recovery program, creating designated court docket sessions to help individuals achieve compliance with the Bureau of Motor Vehicles and obtain valid driver's licenses with insurance. Over a dozen participating veterans have completed community service hours at the park, and some have continued volunteering beyond their required service.

One community business that is frequently called upon by the veteran community is Operation Flags of Freedom, a 501(c)(3) organization dedicated to displaying the American flag as a symbol of patriotism and support. In 2011, when Marine Sergeant Dan Patron was killed in Afghanistan, American flags lined his funeral route in Canton, Ohio, from the church to his final resting place. This powerful tribute became a defining moment for the organization, which continues to honor him and all who have served by creating stunning displays of flags.

Operation Flags of Freedom brings hundreds of flags to events to demonstrate love of country and support for the military. Whether it's a golf outing, birthday, grand opening, car show, community event, school game, veteran homecoming, or military wedding, they provide American flags to mark the occasion. Donations and sponsorships help owner Steve Toohey fulfill his mission of promoting patriotism, ensuring that the service and sacrifices of military men and women are remembered, respected, and honored.

A believer in community, the current mayor of Clinton, Ohio, Bud McDaniel, serves as the vice-president of the OVMP board. He enjoys the charm of small-town living, stating, "We don't have a lot in this little village, but what we do have is the Ohio Veterans Memorial Park. I often refer to it as the best-kept secret in Northeastern Ohio." According to McDaniel, this status is both a blessing and a drawback. On one hand, it helps protect the park from potential vandalism by those who might not appreciate its significance. On the other, it means that many, who would value the park's tribute to the sacrifices made for the country, may not even know it exists. Despite being the third smallest village in Summit County, "Clinton," he said, "is proud to offer this important and moving attraction."

Some of the earliest and most steadfast supporters of the OVMP have been its photographers. Through their images, they have been able to tell the park's story, capturing powerful moments that convey deep messages. Many of these photographers have generously donated their time and talents over the years.

Dan Draiss of Dan Draiss Photography was one of the first photographers to document the park in its early years. Nearly two decades ago, he began capturing beautiful and poignant images that continue to resonate. With an eye for what matters most to the veteran experience, Dan pays attention to every meaningful detail, ensuring that the spirit of the park shines through.

Cliff Franks of Buckeye Drone has highlighted the park from a different perspective, using drone photography and videography to capture stunning aerial views, both in the summer and winter. His creative videos, available on YouTube, not only document events but also showcase the park's serene beauty throughout the seasons, rain or shine. Cliff's dedication extends beyond scheduled events—he can often be found filming on quiet weekdays, driven by a genuine passion for the park's overall aesthetics. Many of the still shots used in the park's materials are taken directly from his video footage.

Steve Wallis of Steve's My Dream Photo has been a reliable presence at the park over the past few years, always just a phone call away for events both large and small. His blend of technical skill and artistic vision has allowed him to breathe new life into old, faded photos from the 1960s, restoring them without losing the natural feel of the original images. Many of his shots have been used for advertising and educational purposes to help to spread the park's message.

The park committee deeply appreciates the contributions of these talented photographers whose work has been instrumental in preserving and sharing the park's story with a wider audience.

Scout groups, including both Boy Scouts and Girl Scouts, have been dedicated volunteers at the OVMP over the years. They have helped with tasks ranging from gathering coins and personal items before deep cleaning the monument to placing new borders and shoveling slate around the walkways. Additionally, the park has been the site of numerous Eagle Scout projects, planned and executed by Boy Scouts aiming to achieve the rank of Eagle Scout—the highest rank in the Boy Scouts of America (renamed Scouting America in 2025). The Eagle Scout charge emphasizes living with honor, the foundation of all character, and these projects have made a lasting impact on the community by preserving and enhancing the veterans' memorial.

One notable Eagle Scout project at the park is the firepit designed for the respectful retirement of U.S. flags. The traditional way to retire a flag is through burning it in a controlled, solemn ceremony followed by the burial of the ashes. This project ensures that this honorable practice can continue at the park, symbolizing respect for the nation's flag and those who served under it. A Scout earned the Eagle rank by completing the interior work of a building, which was later transformed into a store selling park merchandise, an important source of support for the park.

Another recent addition, donated in 2022, is a large, comfortable gazebo. The ceiling of this structure features an Eagle Scout project that visually describes the meaning of the thirteen folds in the American flag during a military funeral. Large frames are attached to the ceiling, each displaying a flag fold, starting with the first fold symbolizing life, and progressing through to the thirteenth, which forms a tight triangle of stars symbolizing In God We Trust. Each ceremonial fold in between carries its own symbolic meaning, representing values and principles cherished by the military and veterans' communities. While not prescribed by the U.S. government, these folds hold deep significance and tradition.

These projects, led by Scouts, are more than just physical additions to the park; they are lasting tributes that honor veterans and preserve important symbols of American values and patriotism.

"Night at the Ohio Vietnam Wall-photo credit Steve Wallis"

Over the years, many groups have volunteered their time at the OVMP, helping to wash the wall, clean the monuments and benches, and even tidy up the windows and dust in the Family of Heroes Hall. Car dealerships like VanDevere and numerous other local businesses have community service programs that encourage their employees to give back, making the park a popular spot for spending a few hours contributing to a meaningful cause. Early mornings are often filled with the sounds of chatting and laughter as volunteers work together.

Survitec, a pioneering survival-technology company, is one of these dedicated groups. With a manufacturing plant just a few miles away, Survitec is a natural fit for a military memorial park as they produce survival equipment for the armed forces. With plants worldwide, they work across maritime, defense, and aerospace sectors, creating products like inflatables and flight suits to reduce risks for sailors and pilots.

During their visits, Survitec employees not only perform deep cleaning at the park but also bring a sense of joy and energy through their time and dedication. The park's volunteers are deeply grateful for the community's ongoing support that helps maintain the park in honor of the fallen heroes it commemorates.

The OVMP is now nearly complete, with upgrades designed to ease care and maintenance. One of the most notable improvements is the use of a robotic lawn mower, which continuously trims the grass, redefining outdoor maintenance for the park's volunteers. This mower meticulously manicures the lawn, creating sharp, clean edges around the walkways with a uniformity and precision any military veteran can appreciate. Once its work is done, it returns to its charging station, ready to power up for the next day. While the robotic mower handles most areas, some of the larger sections are still maintained with a tractor and a volunteer.

Russell Paul Mottmiller is often seen mowing around the perimeter of the park several times a week. Though not a veteran, Russ feels a deep connection to the park and has been a dedicated volunteer since 2018. Living nearby, he spends time at the park almost every day, often alongside John Stevenhagen.

Years ago, when Russ first began volunteering, he told Gary, "I got your back." And he's proven that statement true ever since. From working on the gas lines for the eternal flame to setting up events and guiding school children on tours with engaging stories, Russ's involvement has been invaluable. His dedication has not gone unnoticed—he is a cherished and appreciated member of the park's community.

Each year, Mulch Makers of Ohio, based in Norton, generously donated mulch to the OVMP, which was used around hundreds of feet of tree lines and walkways. While the contribution was greatly appreciated, as the veterans and volunteers of the park have gotten older, the task of shoveling and spreading mulch became more challenging.

To address this, a new plan was implemented: replacing the mulch with a weed barrier and slate rocks. This transition was completed in the fall of 2024 with significant help from the Boy Scouts. While not entirely maintenance-free, the new setup requires much less effort, as the weed barrier effectively reduces weed growth and can be managed with less frequent upkeep. Although the barrier will eventually need to be replaced, the change has made maintenance more manageable for the volunteers.

Over the years, the brick areas near the six military flagpoles began to shift and heave as the poles moved with the wind. Originally, the park's layout included plans for a black granite monument at each flagpole, featuring the emblem and history of each military branch, but this part of the design had yet to be realized.

A decision was made to complete the original vision, and granite was ordered from the same quarry in India that supplied the stone for the park's walls. The bricks near the flagpoles were replaced with new slate, and footers were poured to secure the future granite monuments. These monuments are set to be finished in the spring of 2025.

Chapter Nine

"Creation of the military history monuments to be placed at each flagpole. Leah Goodrich and Jessica Sampsel at work in the shop-photo credits Ken Noon, Summit Memorials, Inc"

The dream of owning a Huey helicopter was realized as well and will be displayed in the spring of 2025. It was obtained from a seller in Texas. The excitement is palpable in the Vietnam veterans at the park. Chuck stated, "We have been trying to get one for seventeen years! It will pull a lot of people to the park as well as every living Vietnam vet. I hoped to still be here to see it." Gary exclaimed, "It will mean something very special to any veteran who has heard the distinctive *WOP-WOP-WOP* of those blades coming through the jungle to pick them up from harm's way."

"New and final acquisition at the park: Huey helicopter-photo credit Steve Wallis"

The installation will not only include a dedication ceremony but also a celebration, as the monuments at the flagpoles and the addition of the Huey mark the completion of the park's long-held plans, bringing the vision for the OVMP to its full realization.

Public recognition and remembrance at veteran memorials play a crucial role in the healing process, while offering opportunities to honor veterans and their sacrifices. Memorial events and tributes also serve as a bridge of reconciliation, particularly for Vietnam War veterans, acknowledging that all wars bring suffering.

Veteran parks reinforce core values like loyalty, courage, and self-sacrifice, which are integral to our national character. Remembering the efforts of soldiers is not just an act of respect; it is an expression of solidarity and a way to stay connected to these enduring values.

Veterans' memorial parks have become a growing phenomenon across Ohio over the last decade, from small villages to county seats. One notable example is Settlers' Watch, part of the Second Street Garden Project in Lorain, where an eagle carved from a tree stands in tribute to Eric Barnes, a fallen airman whose story has been shared in these pages.

Chapter Nine

War memorials throughout Ohio vary widely, ranging from traditional American Civil War cannons and lone statues in town centers to more unique tributes, such as a plot of land near Columbus, the state capital, devoted to the War on Terrorism. These memorials, diverse in form and scale, all serve as powerful reminders of the sacrifices made by service members.

The Ohio Fallen Heroes Memorial, established in June 2005, is a dedicated tribute founded by local veterans from Sunbury, Ohio, in Delaware County. Veterans from VFW Post 8736 and American Legion Post 457 envisioned creating a beautiful memorial to honor all men and women in uniform from Ohio who have made the ultimate sacrifice defending our country in the Global War on Terrorism since September 11, 2001.

"Crosses at night at the Ohio Fallen Heroes Memorial in Sunbury, Ohio-with permission of the Ohio Fallen Heroes Memorial"

As a nonprofit organization, the memorial relies on donations and fundraising events to support and maintain the park. The property is graced by 293 marble crosses, each representing a fallen hero who lost their life while deployed in a combat zone during the Global War on Terrorism. The first cross that was placed honors the first Ohio veteran who died in Iraq, and the most recent cross commemorates a veteran who died during the evacuation of the airport in the withdrawal from Afghanistan.

Each year, a ceremony is held on the Saturday closest to 9/11, offering a solemn occasion to remember and honor these fallen heroes. The sight of the marble crosses is a powerful and moving tribute, reflecting the courage and sacrifice of those who gave their lives in service to their country.

One of the most impressive and innovative tributes to veterans in Ohio is Patriots Park in Amherst, Lorain County. This project is the creative vision of the Veterans Mural Association, a group of dedicated American patriots who have sponsored a series of breathtaking murals honoring the military. Towering works of art on the side of a large brick building vividly depict iconic images from various conflicts, powerfully honoring the sacrifices of servicemen and women.

Chapter Nine

"Patriots Park, Amherst, Ohio; mural artist Michael Sekletar -with permission of John Sekletar"

The project began with Navy veteran John Sekletar, whose talented artist son Michael once approached him with a request: "Dad, can you find a building that I can paint a mural on? It needs to be big. It will be the Marines raising the flag on Iwo Jima." After making inquiries around town, John secured the perfect site, and the building owner readily agreed since there was no cost involved. After funds were raised, the first mural, depicting the famous Iwo Jima flag-raising, was completed in 2011.

"It's become my passion," John stated proudly. The Iwo Jima mural features a real flagpole extending thirteen feet above the building, topped with a replica forty-eight-star flag to maintain authenticity. "I had to come up with a way to get that pole at a perfect angle to the painting," he recalled.

Over the next thirteen years, the project grew in ways that amazed even John. "The most heartwarming aspect," he said, "has been the community coming together to support the endeavor." Three additional murals have since been added to the side of the two-story brick building, each capturing different aspects of military service.

Adjacent to the murals, a new outdoor art museum has been established to further showcase military-themed artwork. Eleven different commissioned pieces are displayed year-round on a sandstone wall, chosen to reflect the local heritage—Amherst and South Amherst, known as the "Sandstone Center of the World," has a rich history of sandstone quarries. This wall serves as a frame for artwork created by local artists, celebrating the strength, resilience, and humanity of soldiers.

"Patriots Park, Amherst, Ohio; sandstone gallery-
with permission of John Sekletar"

Each Veterans Day, these works of art are rotated out and replaced with new paintings, ensuring a fresh display and continued promotion of the arts in the area. During the unveiling ceremony, the stories behind each piece are shared and recognition is given to both the artists and the honored veterans.

"People want to help. They volunteer time and money to support us. They get involved. And we get hundreds of people for Veterans Day. It's just wonderful!" John said. Veterans Day has become the park's signature event, drawing large crowds each year. In recent years Patriots Park has earned awards from the Veterans Day National Committee in recognition of its efforts to honor veterans and host memorable celebrations.

In the village of Smithville, Wayne County, a memorial has been built within the village's park system, serving as a tribute to those who have served. A walkway leads to an American flag, surrounded by five monuments representing each branch of the military. The paving bricks along the path are engraved with the names of servicemen and women, honoring their dedication and sacrifice.

Beautifully designed and thoughtfully placed, the memorial preserves the legacy of service, encourages a sense of civic duty, and ensures that future generations remain connected to the past and the values these soldiers upheld.

A new veterans park, which has been in the planning stages for over ten years, is scheduled for completion and its dedication in the spring of 2025 in Norton, Summit County. "I believe that every town across the country should honor our veterans in some way," said Jamie Lukens, an Army veteran and member of the Norton city council, who is spearheading the project. "I have friends who fought in Afghanistan, including one who was severely injured. We can't forget what they have done for us."

3095 Plus: Ohio's Fallen

The memorial will feature several meaningful monuments along a winding pathway leading to the American flag and monuments at the various flags of the military branches. Like many veterans' parks across the country, the community is raising funds by selling commemorative bricks and accepting donations. Ruth Stimac, who has served on the Parks & Cemetery Board in Norton for most of the past three decades, recalled when the idea was first proposed. "It's so great to see the momentum building to finally get the veterans park finished."

"The POW statue for the park in Plain Township, Ohio; designed and carved by Ken Noon-Photo credit Ken Noon, Summit Memorials"

In 1972, when Kathy Strong was twelve years old, she asked for a bracelet for Christmas. At the time, many seventh graders wore the popular POW/MIA silver bracelets, a trend that started as a way to remember American prisoners of war in Southeast Asia during the Vietnam War. This movement began in the late 1960s when the wives of missing pilots sought to raise awareness about the plights of their

Chapter Nine

husbands. They reached out to a group of college students who formed Voices in Vital America, and the POW/MIA Bracelet Campaign was born.

Most of the bracelets were nickel-plated, each engraved with the name, rank, and capture or missing date of a soldier. When POWs returned home in 1973, people continued to wear the bracelets to honor those still listed as missing in action, intending to keep them on until those soldiers were found or returned. Kathy received one in her Christmas stocking that year, and she wore it for thirty-eight years.

The name on Kathy's bracelet was "Spec 5 James Moreland, 2-7-68." As it turned out, he was killed in action that day, but his body was not recovered. Kathy, along with Moreland's family, did not know this. On the twentieth anniversary of his MIA date, she contacted her local newspaper to share the story of the bracelet. On the fortieth anniversary, she wrote another article, which gained nationwide attention due to the Internet. That year in 2008, James Moreland's sister Linda saw her story and reached out to Kathy who then traveled to Washington state to meet Linda and her sister Anita.

Three years later, Kathy received word from the family that James Moreland's remains had been found and identified. His funeral was held in 2011, and Kathy attended along with hundreds of others who paid their respects, either at the service or along the procession route. During the service, she placed the bracelet she had worn for thirty-eight years in the casket with his remains and uniform, replacing it with a button bearing his name that she now wears on her shirt. She is on a mission.

This is where the OVMP comes in. In October of 2022, Ohio became the twenty-fifth state that Kathy Strong visited to place a brick with James Moreland's name on it to memorialize him. She was interviewed by board member and Vietnam veteran Bob McCullough who met her at the OVMP where she placed the brick. Bob wrote a heartfelt article about her story. Since 2011, Kathy has been traveling to one veterans' memorial park in each state to dedicate a brick to James Moreland. When asked why she chose OVMP over other memorial parks in Ohio, she told Bob that the park seemed to genuinely honor and pay tribute to POW/MIA veterans. She was halfway through her mission to memorialize James in all fifty states.

"The Christmas tree loved by visitors-photo credit Steve Wallis"

The hero's journey often begins with an ordinary life, where an individual is called to adventure and tested through resistance and conflict. This journey pushes them to their limits, where they might be tempted to give up or give in. The soldier embodies the best of human character, balancing duty with moral responsibility and standing as a symbol of the values they defend. They are our heroes.

The journey of the memorial park's builders mirrors this heroic path. They set out to honor these heroes, facing their own challenges along the way. Finding suitable property was difficult, and

Chapter Nine

many doubted the project, lacking faith in the cause or the group's abilities to succeed. Yet, through hard work, harsh weather, personal disagreements, and a range of differing ideas, they persevered. They confronted obstacles without fear, resisted self-doubt despite significant setbacks, and maintained unwavering motivation when faced with physical, emotional, and psychological barriers. To them, failures were not defeats but opportunities for feedback, prompting them to refine their approaches and seek creative solutions. Despite personal flaws, high costs, and opposition from those who seemed intent on avenging perceived wrongs, the veterans' resolve remained steadfast.

However, they did not make this journey alone. Community support was crucial in overcoming adversity. Family, friends, and peers provided encouragement, practical help, and financial assistance. True to their original mandate, the park has never received governmental funds, relying instead on the strength and generosity of those who believed in the cause.

Now the park is near completion, letting go should be easy. However, the deep connection to this place runs through the veins of the veterans and volunteers who have poured their time and effort into it. Building the park has become more than just a project—it has become a part of their identity, a source of comfort, and a home.

As construction comes to an end, a new kind of growth begins. This space, once filled with the energy of creation, will now offer the opportunity to rest, reflect and share the fruits of their labor. Though the work is done, the impact remains, and there is still more ahead—moments of peace, connection, and the fulfillment of seeing their vision come to life.

This story is dedicated to the 3,095 fallen Vietnam soldiers from Ohio, whose names are engraved. Plus, it is dedicated to the names of

Ohio fallen from Korea to the War on Terrorism carved on this black granite wall that has two fronts. It is for the families who visit the names and for the builders and caretakers who have made this place possible.

This park stands as a triumph, a testament to an unwavering commitment to never forget or forsake the ideal that it is our sacred duty to recognize, remember, and honor our veterans and their families—now and for generations to come.

"Family remembering loved ones-photo credit Steve Wallis"

CHAPTER NINE

"Standing at the wall-OVMP archives"

Early in the morning, John is at the park, relighting the eternal flame that is often blown out by high winds and rain. "I'm eternally lighting it," he joked. "It's a problem in the gas line. We will sort it out one day. The important thing is that the flame is there for everyone to see, every day." Nearby, Russ is already at work, mowing around the tank. As the sun rises, John bends down and pulls a weed from the brick walk as he walks away.

Notes

Chapter 1

1. Maria Lindsey, "New Franklin chosen for memorial park," *South Side News Leader* 11, no. 29 (2006).

2. Maria Prinzo, "Memorial will be in Clinton," *Akron Beacon Journal*, January 23, 2007.

Chapter 2

1. Sandra Dreurey, "The Clinton Story," unpublished manuscript, 1991.

2. Joseph Campbell, *The Hero with a Thousand Faces* (New World Library, 1990), 40.

3. Jim Flynn, "October 18, 1968: Ambush of the Dough Boys," *Light Horse Air Cavalry* (blog), October 28, 2001, www.lighthorseaircav.com/rpt-flynn-doughboys-18-10.htm.

4. Ann Kagarise, "Clinton Veterans Memorial is a tribute all who have served," *The Suburbanite*, May 10, 2009.

5. Ann Kagarise, "Groundbreaking held at Vietnam Memorial Park," *The Suburbanite*, September 3. 2007

6.. Joe Follansbee, "Arsenal: The river patrol boat was the backbone of the Brown Water Navy," *Vietnam Magazine*, December 15, 2019.

Chapter 3

1. Hobart M. King, "Granite: What is Granite? What is Granite Used For?" Geology.com, accessed January 13, 2025, https://geology.com/rocks/granite.shtml.

2. "United States: war fatalities 1775–2024," Statista, accessed July 4, 2024, https://www.statista.com/markets/411/topic/2293/historical-data/#overview.

3. Bill Lilley, "Monument to Vietnam vets," *Akron Beacon Journal*, January 9, 2009.

4. Melissa Griffy Seeton, "Lest We Forget," *The Canton Repository*, May 5, 2009.

5. Brian Albrecht, "More than just a wall," *The Plain Dealer*, May 11, 2009.

6. Kathy Antoniotti, "Memorial Wall hails Ohio vets of Vietnam War," *Akron Beacon Journal*, May 18, 2009.

7. "First Lieutenant Sharon Ann Lane," The Army Historical Foundation, accessed September 10, 2024, https://armyhistory.org/first-lieutenant-sharon-ann-lane.

Chapter 4

1. Bob Dyer, "Bob Dyer: 'Your Favorite Columnist' bids farewell after 36 years," *Akron Beacon Journal*, November 29, 2020.

2. Dyer, "Akron's tastelessness to last forever," *Akron Beacon Journal*, October 5, 2009.

3. Dyer, "New words for the Akron Bench," *Akron Beacon Journal*, November 3, 2009.

4. Dyer, "Infighting mars park for visitors," *Akron Beacon Journal*, December 15, 2009.

5. Letters to the editor, "Rossi speaks out," *The Suburbanite*, December 20, 2009.

6. Dyer, "Feuding scars veterans' memorial," *Akron Beacon Journal*, January 10, 2010.

7. Ann Kagarise, "A war over the Wall brews in Clinton," *The Suburbanite*, December 13. 2009.

8. Letters to the editor, "Ohio Vietnam Veterans' Memorial being hijacked," *The Suburbanite*, January 10, 2010.

9. Letters to the editor, "Rossi speaks out on Clinton Ohio Veterans Memorial Park Wall issue; so does the memorial committee." *The Suburbanite*, December 20, 2009.

10. Rochelle Rossi, "Ohio Vietnam Veterans Memorial Park," Veterans-For-Change, December 21, 2009, https://veterans-for-change.tripod.com.

11. Davis, comments by Rochelle Rossi, "Ohio Vietnam Veterans' Memorial being hijacked," *Canada Free Press*,

December 28, 2009, https://canadafreepress.com/article/ohio-vietnam-veterans-memorial-being-hijacked.

12. Davis, email message to Summit Memorials requesting to dismantle the OVMP board, December 23, 2009.12.

13. Dyer, "Light shines on fight in Clinton," *Akron Beacon Journal*, October 26, 2010.

Chapter 5

1. "United States: war fatalities 1775–2024," Statista, https://www.statista.com/markets/411/topic/2293/historical-data/#overview.

2. Dave Roos, "6 Iconic Helicopters Deployed in the Vietnam War," History.com, A&E Television Networks, updated June 20, 2023, https://www.history.com/news/helicopters-vietnam-war.

3. Gayle Tzemach Lemmon, *Ashley's War: The Untold Story of a Team of Women Soldiers on the Special Ops Battlefield* (Harper, 2015), 144.

Chapter 6

1. Ashish Kumar Sen, "Addressing the Harmful Legacy of Agent Orange in Vietnam," United States Institute of Peace, January 27, 2022, https://www.usip.org/publications/2022/01/addressing-harmful-legacy-agent-orange-vietnam.

2. Theresa Cottom, "Unveiling Brings Surprise Tribute," *Akron Beacon Journal*, November 13, 2017.

3. Jim Carney, "Honoring the fallen," *Akron Beacon Journal*, August 29, 2013.

4. "D-Day Facts, Significance & More," Veteran.com Community, Three Creeks Media, updated June 6, 2024, https://veteran.com/d-day/.

5. "The Purple Heart" (PDF), U.S. Department of Veterans Affairs, https://www.va.gov/opa/publications/celebrate/purple-heart.pdf.

6. "Missing Man Table," War Memorial Center, accessed January 13, 2025, https://warmemorialcenter.org/missing-man-table/.

7. "Honors for Valor," U.S. Department of Defense, Defense Media Activity, accessed January 13, 2025, https://www.defense.gov/Multimedia/Experience/honors-for-valor/.

8. "POW MIA," U.S. Department of Defense, Defense Media Activity, accessed January 13, 2025, https://www.defense.gov/Multimedia/Experience/POW-MIA/.

9. Carney, "Statue honors our Gold Star Fathers," *Akron Beacon Journal*, May 12, 2014.

Chapter 7

1. Patrick Sammon, "A Marine's sacrifice," *Vietnam Magazine*, December 2004.

2. Anna Stecewycz, "Portion of Route 93 honors New Franklin Marine killed in Vietnam War," *The Suburbanite*, August 4, 2017.

3. "M60 Patton Tank," First Division Museum, accessed January 13, 2025, https://www.fdmuseum.org/exhibit/m60-patton-tank/.

4. "The Medal," The National Medal of Honor Museum Foundation, accessed January 13, 2025, https://mohmuseum.org/the-medal/.

5. Jim Fausone, "Rodger 'Fuzz' Young: The True Story of a Weekend Warrior," Home of Heroes: Medal of Honor & Military History, Legal Help For Veterans, accessed January 13, 2025, https://homeofheroes.com/heroes-stories/world-war-ii/rodger-young/.

6. *Collecting Sgt. Dan*, directed by Matt Patron (March 2014).

Chapter 8

1. Bison Books, *The Vietnam War: An Almanac*, (World Almanac Publications, 1980).

2. Joe Swayze, "Mail, Like Dirt and Dying, Has Always Been Part of War," *Octofoil: 9th Infantry Division in Vietnam* 2, no. 3 (1970).

3. Ken Olson, "Vietnam's Combat Trackers," *American Legion Magazine*, April 22, 2013.

4. Susan Merritt, *Seek On! Combat Trackers in Vietnam*, 2nd ed. (CreateSpace, 2018).

5. "Battlefield Cross History," MarineParents.com, accessed January 13, 2025, https://marineparents.com/battlefield-cross-history.asp.

Chapter 9

1. "Number of military fatalities in all major wars involving the United States from 1775 to 2024," Statista, accessed January 27, 2025, https://www.statista.com/statistics/1009819/total-us-military-fatalities-in-american-wars-1775-present/.

2. Jim Carney, "Tech-savvy kids assist memorial park's search," *Akron Beacon Journal*, April 22, 2013

Acknowledgements

Thank you to the fallen veterans for your sacrifice, courage, and dedication. We honor your memory and the legacy of freedom you have left behind. The fallen veterans serve as a bridge between the past and present, ensuring that those who gave everything are not forgotten. Freedom comes at a cost. Every flag-draped coffin is a life once full of promise. Your service will never be forgotten.

Thank you to those who built this park—your dedication and the recounting of your stories were indispensable in the writing of this book.

Thank you to the families of the fallen—the stories of their loved ones, though difficult to share, must be told. We respect those left behind.

Thank you to my editor, Michael Jarnebro, Vigilant Proofreader, LLC, for his expertise, insights, and kindness.

Thank you to Steve Wallis, an OVMP photographer, for his skill and readiness assisting with the book's photographs and cover art.

Thank you to Bob McCullough, a steadfast believer and fellow interviewer. You are much appreciated.

And a big shout out to the many firms, companies, and individuals who volunteered time, goods, and services to build this beautiful place. Many have been mentioned in the text. Many of these have not, though their contributions are equally appreciated:

The Dominion Foundation
County of Summit, Ohio
County of Clermont, Ohio
County of Athens, Ohio
International Brotherhood of Electrical Workers, Local 306
National Brotherhood of Boilermakers & Iron Ship Builders
Summit Memorials Inc.
Akron Paint and Varnish, Inc.
Dave Galloway, Portis Electric
American Veterans, Summit County Chapter 35
Disabled American Veterans
Donald C. Hare
Gage 3D, Inc.
Golden Macaw Sheet Metal, Inc
Graphic Accents
Hillside Park
Ohio Beauty Cut Stone
Ohio Blasting & Media, Inc.
Oser's Dairy and Deli
Robert E. Smith Well Drilling
Swigart Easterling Funeral Home
Tommy Edwards Records
Wolff Brothers Supply, Akron
VFWs, Foreign Legions, and Eagles Clubs throughout the region
Veterans Motorcycle Clubs throughout the region

The warmest thank you to Kenneth C. Noon without whom this book would simply be an idea. It's chock full of his stories. He provided the names of those to be interviewed, the research materials needed, much crucial insight and support. I'm proud to call him a co-author.

Thank You For Reading Our Book

We really appreciate all of your feedback and
We love hearing what you have to say.

We need your input to make the next version of this
book (and our future books) better.

Please take two minutes now to leave a helpful review on
Amazon letting us know what you thought of the book.

Thanks so much!

— Erin & Ken

www.ingramcontent.com/pod-product-compliance
Lightning Source LLC
Chambersburg PA
CBHW071154160426
43196CB00011B/2075